"This is *Field of Dreams* meets *The Road to Damascus*, a blend of baseball and belief—at times humorous, at times poignant—that is neither sacrilegious nor shallow. Just as understanding baseball at its deepest levels helps us appreciate the game, so does *Sermon on the Mound* help us appreciate life and the Author of life. Michael O'Connor for Rookie of the Year."

> Bob Welch—Author of *Stories From the Game of Life* & *A Father For All Seasons*

"Isn't it ironic that a human error in baseball contributed to Michael O'Connor winning the most important game of his life by accepting Jesus Christ as his Savior. In baseball, practicing makes us better. In real life 'practicing His presence' continually puts us in position to lead others to Jesus and enables us to live a life of joy and contentment. As the Bible declares, 'In His presence is fullness of joy.' Michael and his wife, Sally, know that by surrendering to Him, they have won life's equivalent to the World Series!"

> Gene Pemberton—Chaplain, Houston Astros

"What I know about baseball wouldn't even fill a catcher's mitt. But I know good writing—make that gorgeous writing. Michael O'Connor knows how to make words sing, and sing they do in *Sermon on the Mound*. His prose is lyrical, his message, novel. I'm a voracious reader, yet there are only a few writers today whom I place in the 'excellent' category: Anne Lamott, Frank McCourt, Annie Dillard, Pat Conroy, and John McPhee. To that list, I now add Michael O'Connor."

> Laura Jensen Walker—Author of *Thanks for the Mammogram* & *Dated Jekyll, Married Hyde*

"Michael O'Connor crafts each word with the disciplined grace of a poet—albeit one who is clutching a hot dog and spilling a Coke as he roars 'SLIDE!' at the guy heading for third base. *Sermon on the Mound* will leave you whispering, 'Thank God for baseball.' And if you listen closely, you'll hear 'You're welcome.'"

> Dave Meurer—Author of *Boyhood Daze* & *Daze of Our Wives*

"Michael O'Connor knows how to turn a phrase. His description of America's favorite pastime is delivered with the precision of a Catfish Hunter and all the flamboyance of a Randy Johnson. You'll have to decide for yourself whether *Sermon on the Mound* is a baseball book about spirituality or a spiritual book about baseball. Either way, it's a grand slam."

> David Brickner—Executive Director, Jews For Jesus

SERMON
ON THE
MOUND

Sermon on the Mound
Copyright © 2001, 2005
Michael O'Connor

Cover and interior design by Dan Thornberg
Typesetting by Aaron Sharar

Cover photo and photos of Don Larsen on pages 9 and 171 © Bettmann/CORBIS.
Cover photo: Colorized photo of New York Yankee Don Larsen pitching his perfect
game against the Brooklyn Dodgers in the 1956 World Series. © Bettmann/CORBIS.

Photos of Mickey Mantle on p. 7 and others, Babe Ruth on p. 106, and the Cleveland
Indians on p. 122 are courtesy of the National Baseball Hall of Fame Library,
Cooperstown, New York.

Photo of New York Mets on p. 130 by T. J. Higgins/Allsport

Photo of Don Drysdale on p. 148 © Bettmann/CORBIS

Published by Bethany House Publishers
11400 Hampshire Avenue South
Bloomington, Minnesota 55438

Bethany House Publishers is a division of
Baker Publishing Group, GrandRapids, Michigan.

Printed in the United States of America

ISBN 0-7642-2395-X (Hard cover)

Library of Congress Cataloging-in-Publication Data

O'Connor, Michael, 1955–
    Sermon on the mound : finding God at the heart of game / by Michael
O'Connor.
        p.   cm.
    ISBN 0-7642-2913-3
    1. Christian life. 2. Baseball—Religious aspects—Christianity. I. Title.
    BV4501.2 .O3235 2005
    248.8'8—dc21

                                                      00-012157

MICHAEL O'CONNOR

SERMON ON THE MOUND

FINDING GOD AT THE HEART OF THE GAME

BETHANYHOUSE

MINNEAPOLIS, MINNESOTA

Dedication

Legend has it that Babe Ruth, for the benefit of a sick little boy, once pointed to the outfield bleachers as he stepped up to the plate and "called" the home run he proceeded to hit. Bravado of this sort works better for athletes than it does for writers. Instead, as I stand for the first time in this strange new batter's box, I step out for just a moment, turn, and point to my parents, Charles and Dorothy. Their unified pride in their firstborn son and their unwavering support of his dreams gave me the confidence and the time to find the things I do well.

This swing is for you, Mom and Dad.

Acknowledgments

Really fine baseball is a product of dedication and teamwork. It truly never occurred to me that writing a book is the same, until I became immersed in this project and realized how much I needed my community. I want to express my admiration and gratitude for the contributions of my brothers and sisters:

Michael and Laura Walker—Who had me over to their home one night for a brainstorming session. What would I write about, they wondered, if I could create whatever meant the most to me? "That's easy," I replied. "I'd write about my two favorite subjects— God and baseball." I then proceeded to explain how silly was the notion of throwing these two dissimilar ingredients into the same kettle, but they kept interrupting me. They said it was an amazing concept. I told them no one would believe my crazy theory that God loves baseball. I spent the next ten minutes trying to talk them out of my idea. I lost the argument. This is the absolute truth: All the Walkers needed to do was say, "Next," and this book would not have been written. This is all their fault.

Steve Laube—Senior Editor with Bethany House Publishers. Steve, himself a rabid sports fan, caught the vision for this book and went to bat for *Sermon on the Mound* with the editorial and marketing teams. As God began revealing stories long forgotten, the direction of this book began changing. Steve gave me more latitude to explore this new path than any rookie author has a right to expect. "Write the best book that God has given you" was his admonition.

Dave Talbott and Staff—Host and Director at the amazing Mt. Hermon Christian Writers Conference. This symposium changed my life. It opened up a world of possibilities to a novice writer who needed prayer, encouragement, and solid foundational knowledge in the realm of Christian publishing. For any Christian writer with a call or vision, this is the place where dreams can come true.

David and Heather Kopp—Whose Mt. Hermon workshop on writing nonfiction books had a significant impact on the acceptance of my book proposal. Writers would do well to sit at the feet of these wonderful teachers.

Christopher Soderstrom—God sent a ram to Abraham as a sign there would be no cutting. Bethany House sent Christopher as line editor for this volume to signify there would be very little. I prayed the work would be done by someone who understood the intricacies of baseball, who also possessed an empathy for the underlying pain of birthing a book. God sent me a Minnesota Twins fan. Who would know better about pain? His camaraderie and passion for the game were an answer to prayer.

Bill Dwyer and Lynn Cory—I have been blessed to call these men "Pastor" for fifteen years and am excited about the next fifteen. So much of who I am in Christ is born through the very human examples these gifted teachers and humble men live out as the arms of Jesus.

Joe Falls, Jim Murray, Dave Kindred, Wells Twombly, and Roger Angell—These are the men I grew up reading. These are the men who opened my eyes and convinced me that sportswriting could be more than scores and facts—it could be literature.

Max Shulman and Jean Shepherd—The humorists. Max taught me the joys of whimsy and Jean blessed me with a love for rich, descriptive language. Their influence is perpetual in my life and writing. They deserve to be read by new generations starving for laughter. Find them and read them well.

John Fischer—Author, musician, theologian, baseball fan (though not necessarily in that order). John is a Renaissance man who loves God and the Anaheim Angels. I am grateful for his willingness to say a few words to open this book and for his generous, kindred spirit in discussions on writing and the game we both love.

The Prayer Warriors—There are far too many to name and still have pages for the book. Their devotion has been steadfast, their intercession essential. When grace rained down on me during the hardest chapters, I knew these men and women were standing strong, holding up my wavering arms, which seemed at times too weary to reach for another key. May God bless your faithful hearts.

The Readers—Kevin and Annette Grable, who scoured my lines for grammatical misdemeanors and felony commas. Also Mary Trahan, who critiqued many pieces and made late-night runs for Diet Coke and Tommy's Burgers; and Lynn Shilman, who was a great listener whenever I needed to see how something worked aloud. Finally, thanks to Scott Rubin, Marty Walker, and Cindy-Dawne Kotzen, who offered encouragement and advice at the outset of the project.

The Rose Garden Inn, Santa Maria, California, Room 210— The place where much of this book was written. There are far too many beautiful women in my house for a man to concentrate on writing. This haven near the California coast provided shelter and privacy at amazing rates during my five or six extended stays with them. Blessings to Kathy and Mary.

Dave Shilman—Whose simple encouragement kept me going. "In heaven," he continually offered, "this book is already a done deal."

Betty Klein—My wife's mother who, as she lay dying, and understanding my poor track record for completing projects I start, weakly pointed her finger and said to me, "You *finish* this book." It was more a warning than an admonishment. Such was the spunk of this fine lady. I miss you, Mommy-law.

Dusty Rose and Bonnie Joy—Daughters both, you are my great treasure from the Lord. Too much time was lost between us because Daddy had to stay up late. I finally got a 9-to-5 job, and it turned out to be during your bedtime. Let's go miniature golfing soon.

Sally Klein O'Connor—My wife, my love, my Beauty. You fit under almost every category above. Except that you are not a motel. What you are is a rock. During the hardest period of your life, having lost your mother and father in the same year, having to deal with health issues that put our music ministry on hold, you were the one who looked me in the eye and told me I could finish. You were the one who covered my responsibilities at home. You were the one who without complaint edited tirelessly every word I wrote and allowed me to share portions of your very personal journal. You were the one. You *are* the one.

Table of Contents

Foreword

by John Fischer

I wouldn't have believed it if he hadn't just brought an audience to tears through the eloquence and depth of his words. I was at a writer's conference when I first met Michael O'Connor. He read an award-winning poem the same night I gave a keynote address, part of which connected spiritual insights to certain aspects of the game of baseball. Around a table later that evening, Michael let me know he shared my bent for the national pastime, and in particular, he revealed how his conversion to Christianity was directly related to the failure of the Boston Red Sox to take Game Six of the 1986 World Series, when, more times than any Red Sox fan chooses to remember, they had the New York Mets on the ropes.

I had two choices. I could dismiss the man as a lunatic or listen to his story. Extenuating circumstances compelled me to listen. You see, I was one of those fans who will never forget being glued to my TV set while that particular game unraveled before my eyes. I lived thirty-five miles north of Boston at the time and had followed that team all year right up to the bitter end, and it was indeed bitter. Was this man going to now tell me, twelve years later, that something good had come out of that bumbling play that ended the game in the bottom of the tenth? Did the same voice from *Field of Dreams* send him to me with a mandate to ease my pain?

If you believe in God and/or baseball, you will listen too, because now, in a longer form, you have the story here in your hands where you can savor it like a long afternoon at the ballpark. Then you can decide for yourself if God can be in these things. I, for one, am a believer.

And why not? Why couldn't God use baseball for eternal purposes completely unknown to those churning out their plays day after day on an emerald diamond? Why couldn't He be using it for a million and one things in a million and one people's lives all at the same time? After all He is God; He can do stuff like this.

There are other stories here besides Michael's conversion, and stories within stories. This is where Michael's writing takes us beyond baseball, for if God can be seen behind the scenes of a ball game or a long season of play, how many other things is He using in all of our lives to get our attention?

Will we ever know how complex and delicate these lines are with which He holds us and our faith together and draws us to Him? What are these ties that bind? Will we ever get to the end of them?

Whatever you think about the compatibility or incompatibility of God and baseball, I urge you to suspend your judgment and read. Don't try to figure out if this is God or coincidence. Just let the stories soak in like a rained-out doubleheader. You may just start finding God when and where you least expect Him, and long after you put this book down.

—John Fischer

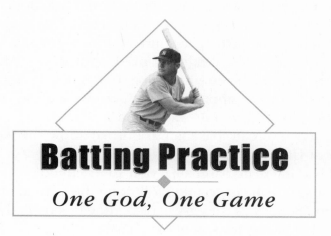

Batting Practice

One God, One Game

I believe in two things. God the Father, Son, and Holy Spirit, Creator of heaven and earth, the beginning and the end, the Alpha and Omega, the one and only Source from which all life flows—and baseball.

Everything else is just sports and religion.

You see, baseball is not simply a sport. The game is a celebrated rite of passage through the corridors of our youth; a game whose long, rich history allows us to retrace those early steps at any point in the journey. Despite the abundant evidence of the worshiping masses, baseball is neither a faith unto itself nor a holy altar to fall prostrate upon while offering burnt sacrifices in exchange for a play-off berth. But make no mistake. Baseball is an awesome trust and a sacred privilege—one I believe God somehow had a hand in creating.

How many times in life are you permitted—no, *invited*—to witness a miracle carved from the simple, hardened beauty of a perfect diamond? When do you know you've studied at da Vinci's feet and gazed into the eyes of Mona Lisa? How often do you open your heart to a symphony of howling humanity and weep— *weep* at the realization there may be no more beautiful music in creation? Oh, yeah…every time you go to the ballpark.

If someone besides God created baseball, I have yet to see evidence that would hold up in court. History, depending to which version you subscribe, credits Abner Doubleday or Alexander Cartwright with the game's invention. But I know better. One of those guys may have applied for the permits and laid the foundation, but God inspired the blueprint.

God had to create baseball, if only to show the world He hadn't lost His touch.

God had to create baseball, if only to reach me.

Revealing His heart to mine following the sixth game of the 1986 World Series was the easy part. Getting Boston Red Sox fans to accept His Divine Intrusion was quite another. That, however, is clearly another story for another chapter.

———◆———

At fifteen I left the church I was part of because it had nothing more to offer me. I had grown wary of the rituals of religion that seemed to be in place more to obscure than to reveal the presence of God. I was never encouraged to read the Bible. I was taught to fear God. No one ever talked of knowing or loving Him. I felt no connection with my Maker and only vaguely acknowledged Him as such. So leaving was easy.

Organized religion, ironically, had a hand in my spiritual undoing. I think God is as comfortable with religion as the Rockettes are in Levi's. That's because, although He is interested in our buildings, our financial stewardship, our liturgy—all those things that hold an appropriate place within the fellowship and kingdom of God—He's not hung up on them. God is primarily concerned with *relationship*. He loves *us*, not our stuff. He longs for us to return to Him that same love.

Now for a small confession: I often enjoy watching football on television. I have even been known to point my remote in the direction of the NBA Finals on occasion. Yet while it's true I find these other sports intriguing, even enjoyable, I have never found a means within their finite structures or parameters to help bring definition to my existence, much less clarity to my soul.

Baseball does this for me. Thankfully, to a far greater degree, so does God.

Like God, baseball has always focused on relationship. Owner to manager. Manager to player. Player to fan. It is as simple as fathers playing catch with their sons and as complex as a ball smacking the pocket of a well-oiled glove that echoes and ripples throughout generations. There is a wealth of history and lore in baseball that is simply unequaled in our other modern-day sports. Novelist Bernard Malamud knew this. "The whole history of baseball," he wrote, "has the quality of mythology."

Malamud was right. Baseball is a game of character and characters. It is legendary manager Casey Stengel, gone for thirty years, who remains alive in our hearts and who lifts our spirits as he reminds us, even from the grave, "Good hitting will always stop good pitching, and vice versa." Or former Phillies skipper Danny Ozark, who somehow makes the world seem right and safe as he drops this gem into our collective consciousness: "Half this game is ninety percent mental."*

> *God had to create baseball, if only to show the world He hadn't lost His touch.*

---

* Yes, I know Yogi Berra has also been credited with this remark, but quotes are often incorrectly attributed to him because he's been so...well...quotable. Berra himself admits he has often been cited by writers who invented the remarks attributed to him because they sounded so Berra-esque. So maybe Yogi said this and maybe he didn't. But why should Ozark suffer for having a lousy publicist?

"To compare baseball with other team games," asserts former major-league owner Bill Veeck, "is to say the Hope Diamond is a nice chunk of carbon."

Baseball is utterly unique. It is the only game where, when you are on offense, you never have the ball. The defense does. In football, the team with possession tries to run, pass, or kick the pigskin across a line or between two posts. Giant hoopsters dribble, pass, shoot, and dunk their ball through a metal ring hung ten feet off the ground. Hockey players skate, pass, flip, and slap their puck at a box-shaped target.

In each of these sports, when the pigskin/ball/puck is passed and is intercepted en route to its betrothed, the defense instantaneously becomes an offensive force. The pass picked off by the cornerback is now heading the opposite direction—he has become a running back. Blockers become tacklers. Quarterbacks transform instantly into safeties. All this shifting of employment, just because the ball unexpectedly changed hands.

Not so when the object is small, white, and tightly stitched in red.

In baseball, only one team is fighting for possession. When the ball is hit, the defense scrambles to get it back. Panic ensues when control of it is lost, and the total focus of nine players is dedicated to once more regaining that control and restoring order. How very much like our lives is the pursuit of this wayward sphere.

There we are rattling around in the left-field corner, our once-peaceful existence subverted by a rocket off the bullpen gate. Perhaps that shot comes in the form of feeling a lump where none is supposed to exist. Or the 3:00 A.M. phone call delivering news that your best friend has been badly injured in an automobile accident. Maybe you turn your back in the supermarket for just a moment to grab the bargain box of detergent, and suddenly your three-year-old is nowhere to be found.

There we are chasing down the drive, attempting to keep our cap on straight and smile for the cameras as we misplay the carom, spinning back around toward the plate, trying not to sweat as the ultimate pain—the fear of loss, the fear of *losing*—grabs us by the letters and slams our uniformed body to the ground, a humiliating tumble somewhere between chaos and recovery, that shadowy zone where champions never linger and the outcome remains in doubt.

There we grope on expectant knees to get a handle on the baseball as the batter and lead runner speed ever homeward. There we grovel, spitting out warning-track dust, coaxing the roller to expire in the high grass so we may reclaim it, along with our dignity, just beyond reach.

It is there in that place of poverty, there in our outfield of despair where a hundred thousand eyes plead and pry but cannot relieve us of our solitude—it is in *that place* where God reveals himself to us.

Wise beyond knowing and tender beyond compassion, He dips into a waistband pouch and retrieves an unblemished ball. Holding it in His vast palm, gripping the seams as Walter Johnson or Dizzy Dean surely must have in their day, the Lord cradles this treasure as if it were a gem of the highest value, a jewel whose worth may not be calculated in terms of coin or gold. This ball was plucked from the Tree of Hope, where unbridled gifting and youthful dreams spill their seed to produce such magnificent fruit.

As we reach for the fresh, unspent sphere that holds within it the familiar whiff of springs and autumns played and catalogued, yet somehow still to come, we realize we have no idea what to expect.

Will God yank the treasure back and laugh? Fear sweats the truth out from our souls. Suddenly, we aren't sure we know who God really is. Can He be trusted? Will He renege? Experience in the world has conditioned us to lead with doubt, even if He hasn't.

But a loving father doesn't stick a leg into the aisle to trip his unsuspecting child. And a loving God, even in the midst of an important lesson, derives no joy from our moment of pain. The ball rests in His open palm, ripe for the picking once we get close enough to see it…to feel it…to recognize it. He has not betrayed us.

And when we reach the moment of cognizance, grabbing and gripping the horsehide between four tight fingers and a balancing thumb, the treasure is revealed to be not of silver, nor of gold—but a pearl, and one of great wisdom.

We pump the ball against the soft leather webbing—a wasted motion, really, but one that brings us comfort. As we attempt to straighten our body for the desperate throw to third base, God whispers in our ear what we've learned again and again but our memory banks somehow refuse to retain: *You may have the ball within your glove…you may have the runner within your sights…you may even have the game within your reach…but* I am *ever in control*.

He is not vain or boasting as He shares this, but pointedly matter-of-fact. There is a touch of sadness to His voice. You get the impression He wants us to grasp this fundamental reality, once and for all time.

We throw to the base where the game rests in balance. It is a low bullet that skips once off a blade of grass resting atop a pebble. God knew that tiny rock was there, just as He knows and counts each hair on our head. The impudent stone changes the ball's trajectory imperceptibly but just enough to make the glove on the receiving end waver for a moment—then spill the dream like so much milk on the kitchen floor. An empty mitt applies a clueless tag to a phantom leg. The batter has tripled. The runner at first has scored. The game has been won and lost.

Instantly, we are humbled, not so self-assured as we were coming into the contest. We pick ourselves up again and head for the clubhouse. After a half-hearted kick with a delinquent left cleat, a divot is launched for the groundskeeper to replace. We are more aware than ever that all our God-given talents cannot alone deliver the victory into our hands. We start to understand this is not about *our* hands but infinitely larger and more capable ones.

The Father, with great love, has taken a moment to teach us a far more potent lesson than could be gleaned from the winning of a single game. God has given us a glimpse of a life lived in awe and wonder of Him. The game belongs to God…and so do we.

Even as I began work on this book, the story took on a form and substance very different from my original idea. A lesson seemed to be playing out, independent of my wishes. At first I didn't recognize the teacher, for to do so would be to have admitted I was not in total control; that I was not the master of my young volume's fate. Still, without understanding the ramifications of a diverted path, nor recognizing the subtle touch of God's redirection, new life and fresh vision

> *The game belongs to God…and so do we.*

were breathed between those lines, just as a lifeguard delivers mouth-to-mouth on a swimmer he has rescued from the waters. I found myself in uncharted but vaguely familiar fields of grace until, indeed, this was no longer the tale I set out to write.

Sermon on the Mound had, after all, been plotted and structured around the oddly defensible idea that baseball and the Bible have more in common than many people realize. I wavered momentarily and briefly considered reclaiming my book and its theme by sheer force of will. But a strange and wonderful thing happened.

Strange because it was so totally unexpected.

Wonderful because God was in it.

God began revealing incidents in that part of my personal history that was my baseball past. These were utterly forgotten moments—events securely entombed in mind and heart, forever sealed off by decades of disregard. Should I follow these tiny fragments of bone and clay to their obscure and, no doubt, irrelevant conclusion—or stay the course? *Why,* I muttered internally, *would God commission an archaeological dig to excavate such trivial suburban folklore, soaked in the spit and sweat of silly games from my childhood?*

My first impulse was to leave these memories untouched. That would have been the prudent thing. I had too much work before me to allow a flood of side trips down memory lane—detours that closer examination would surely have encouraged.

But as I was turning my back to walk away from a past that did not seem to warrant revisiting, I noticed a tiny scrap of leather lying neglected in a dusty corner of my subconscious. It could not have comprised more than a square inch of space. Against my better judgment, and despite the fact that it existed solely in the realm of remembrance, I examined the ancient brown remnant. It was surprisingly soft, smooth from years of mental erosion.

I lifted it slowly to my nose. History wafted in, and history smelled like grass. For an instant I was ten years old, standing in right field, holding my glove across the lower portion of my face, peering out above the web while chewing on the mitt's salty leather lace.

I set the fragment aside. I was no longer merely curious but felt compelled to follow the memories wherever they might lead. Were there other mummified secrets to unearth?

With a soft thud, my fingertips hit something larger than the previous discovery. An exposed corner suggested cardboard. My hand brushed some earth aside—strange, how untidy the mind becomes—revealing an old soggy yellowed cigar box. The lid was too decayed to make out the brand name, but the artwork indicated something produced circa 1960. This fantasy, more palpable by the moment, was threatening to swallow me whole.

Removing the top, I found, to my astonishment, contents that were almost entirely preserved in the condition of their latest use. A baseball card…well-centered, with a horizontal crease from edge to edge. The corners were soft, fuzzy nubs—not the crisp, sharp ones you find in a brand-new pack. In its worn condition, the card would be almost worthless in today's market. To me, however, this 1966 Don Drysdale Topps portrait was a priceless find. Curious, though. Why did I even *have* a card of this Hall-of-Fame Dodger pitcher? After all, I grew up a Giants fan.

Exploring further, I noticed a dirty gray shoelace. It was ragged in spots, revealing moderate wear—but it was still in one piece. The plastic tips—you know, those things on both ends of a lace that nobody knows the name of—had long ago abandoned ship, as the frayed nubs testified. But why would I save a shoela—wait a minute! This must be a lace from my P.F. Flyers—the shoes I wore for three straight years in Little League. Why, I was wearing those very shoes that time…the day I tried to steal second base and was thrown out by *thirty feet!*

Next was a ticket stub from 1965. The first big-league game I ever attended. San Francisco. Candlestick Park. Upper deck. Nosebleed section.

Folded in the corner was a newspaper article recounting Game Six of the '86 Mets/Red Sox World Series. The game that changed my life! And look, the team photo from my Babe Ruth Baseball League. There's that coach who never gave me the time of day when time was all I needed. And—holy cow!—a snapshot of me as an adult…leading off of first base. I had just gotten a hit in a softball game.

Each of these relics connected me momentarily to a time and place that was once central to the person I had been so many years before. Relegated for decades to that musty box in my subconscious, they embraced temporary freedom and breathed anew sweet fragrance upon what was once good and right and almost holy about the game I grew up loving.

From that moment on, the landscape of this work changed

from the broad and general thesis that God loves baseball to the immensely deep and personal realization that—more than anything—God loves *me*. As each of these tales was reborn in my heart, I realized with gradual Polaroid clarity how God has used the game of baseball to teach me many of the important lessons in my life. And, eventually, He used the game I love to draw me into a lasting relationship with Him.

These recollections are a miraculous gift from God. I can think of no other reason for their sudden reappearance so many years after they had ceased being relevant. So while these gems were ripe with promise, while the cardboard was still pungent and the moisture of memory hung in the breeze like a slow curve before a .320 hitter, I became their biographer.

It's not as if I really had a choice.

These are the stories as I remember them. It is a privilege to share them with you.

> *Every good and perfect gift*
> *is from above,*
> *coming down from*
> *the Father of the heavenly lights.*
>
> *—James 1:17*

By and large it is the sport that a foreigner is least likely to take to. You have to grow up playing it, you have to accept the lore of the bubble gum card, and believe that if the answer to the Mays-Snider-Mantle question is found, then the universe will be a simpler and more ordered place.

—*David Halberstam*

First Inning

An Affair to Remember

I am having an affair.

My wife knows about it. My children have heard the two of us discussing it in hushed tones from rooms to which they have been exiled. My pastor and many on our church board have brought me in for counseling. Usually people are embarrassed when they find out and don't know what to say.

"Is it so wrong to love?" I ask them. "Is it a sin to follow my heart?" They study the tops of their shoes in silence. But they are not being honest. You can see it in the reflection on their Florsheims. They miss the romance in their lives. They yearn to rekindle the passion. Or perhaps I'm describing something they have never known. Although I have no proof, I believe I am secretly envied.

I am having an affair. It's been going on since Kennedy was president.

The first time I picked up a baseball, it wasn't all that special. The ball was small, round, dirty. I tossed it into the air, and gravity had its way.

I was a kid growing up in a home where the foundation was cracked and the structure was crumbling. Yet here, at last, was something I could depend on. No matter how grass-stained or scuffed was its skin, the ball remained loyal and would always return.

Baseball revealed her inner beauty to me in 1963, and I have been helpless in her presence ever since.

For a time I was a player. But these days I mostly watch. I've learned what brings her joy. I know her flaws and sorrows as if they were my own. I no longer need to be in her presence to be overwhelmed with her fragrance. But it helps. She is not so perfect to me as when I was eight and needy. But she is always beautiful.

I was drawn to this game when I was knee high to a shin guard. Drawn like a pyromaniac to a thatched hut, like an Irishman to a three-day wake. It was almost involuntary.

And though baseball incessantly teased with the promise of pennants and championships, the part of the sport that stressed winning was rarely fulfilling to me. The peaks were generally fleeting, and the valleys went on forever. Not that this mattered. If my lust for victory burned unrequited, I could at least satisfy my burgeoning heart with proximity to the beloved game itself.

God was a different story altogether. If God was calling me during those early days, He got nothing but busy signals. If He was beckoning me to follow, I was on another path. If He was wooing my hungry heart, it was a task requiring supreme perseverance. I was already in love.

To me, God was interesting, mysterious, and worthy of fear. But love—torrid, passionate, fanatical devotion—these are colors of an emotional rainbow I never would have attributed to the Author of all creation. The god I was introduced to was a joyless deity. Mirthless and somber. The one who rained fire and flood upon the land. The one who demanded obedience over and against abiding affection.

I don't know why God didn't strike me dead over this golden calf in the first inning of my existence, why He restrained himself from leveling every baseball diamond from San Diego to Maine in righteous indignation. If my early baseball days were any indication, certainly a lifetime of idolatry lay ahead.

Baseball revealed her inner beauty to me in 1963, and I have been helpless in her presence ever since.

And God had the best seat in the house from which to view this morality play. I marvel how, daily, He must have sat in bemused silence, surprised by nothing, knowing every outcome—peering effortlessly from the press box of eternity through the smoked-glass windows of my soul.

Who would fault Him for growing jealous enough to sift through the corridors of time, delivering plague upon plague to the mid-1800s village of Cooperstown, New York? All God had to do, prior to the game's conception, was send a Bakersfield-sized meteor aimed straight at the heart of its birthplace and baseball is never invented.

Then—poof!—jai alai is America's national pastime.

God had a better idea. It was ingenious, really. Why not take the thing that held my rapt concentration—baseball—and use it to instruct and draw me closer to Him? So brilliant was God's execution, I remained blissfully ignorant of it for the first thirty-one years of my life.

When the day came for Him to reveal this master plan in October of 1986, it grabbed my whole attention like a sharp grounder to short that you expect will hug the ground but instead trick-hops off the hardpan infield, delivering an agonizing shot to your forehead. It's difficult to ignore God when you're flat on your back, seeing stars and counting angels.

◆

The other day a box of old family photographs arrived in the mail. My mother was cleaning out some closets and thought I might enjoy the memories. I found my third-grade class picture and, on a whim, asked my daughter Dusty to pick me out of the lineup. There were sixteen boys in the picture. It took fifteen tries to nail her old man.

> *It's difficult to ignore God when you're flat on your back, seeing stars and counting angels.*

Had I really changed all that much? I guess my twelve-year-old answered that question for me. But it's a little hard to accept. In my heart I am still that third grader, telling the same corny jokes, pulling on little-girl pigtails.

I found a posed snapshot of me taken during my early days of organized ball. The child is slight of build and severely freckled. His short auburn hair is all but hidden by an oversized green cap with a big red *R* on it. His baggy uniform, like Jonah's whale, appears to have swallowed him whole. There is a leather glove carelessly dangling from one hand, appearing to have only decorative value.

You study his eyes and there is a Robinson Crusoe look about them. They are lost and adrift. I guess growing up between the Bay of Pigs and Watergate will do that to you. He is not the vibrant, happy-go-lucky kid I had expected or remembered. Was memory failing or had Mom hired a child actor, purchased her first computer, learned Photoshop, and doctored this picture?

Then it hit me. The red *R* betrayed the mystery. Raineers. This was my first team. My first uniform. My first glove. This was the beginning of the marvelous journey—the start of this lifelong affair. We had, apparently, just met, and infatuation had not yet set in.

Once we became acquainted, baseball gave me purpose and direction. She steered me toward home more times than a designated driver on St. Paddy's Day. Baseball was my salvation—my lithe and graceful partner on the ballroom dance floor of life.

> *Baseball was my salvation—my lithe and graceful partner on the ballroom dance floor of life.*

The boy in the photo doesn't know it yet, but he is about to fall in love. Madly, hopelessly, irrevocably. It will be one of the truly profound miracles in his life.

And isn't it just like God to use a miracle to get our attention?

*Do not lust in your heart
after her beauty
or let her captivate you
with her eyes.*

—*Proverbs 6:25*

You gotta have a catcher or you'll have a lot of passed balls.

—*Casey Stengel*

Second Inning

Glove Story

What can you say about a sixty-four ounce slab of leather that never realized its potential? That it failed in its chosen field? That its manufacturer dropped the ball in production? That it came closer to fulfilling its calling as a doorstop than with a short-stop? These are the questions that haunt my sleep nearly three decades after my brief, undistinguished hardball career.

You could teach a college course on the whys and wherefores of what went wrong with my first glove. Call it Mitt Lit. or Rawlings Scrawlings. Future generations would learn the sorrows I have known on my own private field of dreams, but without perspective, wouldn't they simply be doomed to repeat the same errors?

I share this cautionary tale with you as both warning and primer on what, if at all possible, must be taken into consideration when purchasing a child's first baseball glove. So important is this early consumer decision that it has, no doubt, decided the career of many a potential Hall-of-Famer. Where will the sons of Barry Bonds and Ken Griffey Jr. be without the story of my early playing days available to blaze their respective trails to Cooperstown?

And while we're asking questions, where, indeed, is Fred Wimpleton? Who, you may ask, is Fred Wimpleton? He's a thirty-two-year-old man carving out a tidy career as an all-night clerk at a 7-Eleven store in Grand Junction, Colorado.

Turns out Fred's mother bought his first glove. Her only pre-requisite was that it keep her fragile son's hand warm. In fact, she was such a good mother she bought two fielder's gloves—one for each hand. No telling how far her son, a lanky young man who could spank the ball to all fields, would have gone if his mom had only understood the second baseman's occasional need to throw the ball to first base. On the other hand, Ma Wimpleton is proud of her son in his honest endeavors. To this day he uses the gloves she picked out to avoid freezer burn while stocking the Popsicles and TV dinners. They also, I am told, make excellent ice scrapers during the defrost cycle.

This, then, is my blatant attempt to justify one child's inability to cleanly field a routine grounder, and also to understand for myself that mysterious Bermuda Triangle of the sky that swallowed all those catchable fly balls I never caught. This is my glove story.

◆

When I was about eight, my father bought me a left-handed mitt and began teaching me to play catch. That first fielder's uten-sil was the hardest, flattest thing I had ever seen in my life. I've known manhole covers with more give and curve to them. Neighborhood kids mocked its shape until I had no choice but to join in the derision. Without my dad's knowledge, I affectionately dubbed it "The Pancake."

There was really only one way to encounter incoming objects using The Pancake. First you had to calculate the longitude and latitude through which the ball was due to enter your airspace. Then, with coordinates set, you positioned The Pancake to meet the horsehide head on, like a Bolivian mountainside greeting an incoming jet. You see, The Pancake, unlike most mitts, was never designed to catch balls—only to impede their progress.

All my friends' baseball gloves were like aircraft carriers—latching onto the flying object, bringing it to a sharp and immediate halt. My glove was more like a runway at an abandoned airport—short, full of potholes, begging for demolition. Any ball hit to me would touch down on The Pancake, assault my bony wrist, then roll perilously up my arm. The trick, I had learned, was to stop the ball with my neck before it launched off my shoulder.

Not since Christopher Darden's ill-fated courtroom demonstration has a glove been so out of place on a human hand. One thing was for sure: If there was a Baseball Glove Purchasing Purgatory, my dad was going to be doing some serious time on the rock pile.

> *The Pancake, unlike most mitts, was never designed to catch balls—only to impede their progress.*

It never occurred to me to just ask my dad for a new glove—you know, one you could *catch* a ball with. To this day I believe he must have had some hidden investments in Rawlings that rendered him in-capable of returning The Pancake to our local sporting goods store, lest he spark a stampede of angry, flat-glove-toting parents demanding their money back, sending his precious stock plummeting.

Instead, as evidence of my fielding problems mounted and my taste in candy bars fluctuated from PayDays to Butterfingers, my dad *did* march back into the sporting goods store, investing in a new baseball, a yard of nylon rope, and a small can of baseball glove oil.

I'm not exactly sure what sets baseball glove oil apart from 3-in-1 oil, Quaker State motor oil, or, say, Vitalis—but, according to my father, the properties of this mystical concoction were the magic elixir that The Pancake would need to marinate in before being able to invite a baseball to come in and take up residence. Just as Pinocchio required the touch of the Blue Fairy's wand to complete the transformation from a puppet to a real boy, my dad swore that baseball glove oil would one day make The Pancake a real mitt. The transformation plan was five-pronged.

Step One: Baste the glove in the palm and pocket areas with generous amounts of baseball glove oil, kneading the leather with your hands like a Swedish masseuse working the tension out of a client's back. When this proved to be more work than my father or I had anticipated, we briefly considered hiring an actual Swedish masseuse to visit our home and perform the task for us. However, the cost and zoning laws were prohibitive. So I fastened The Pancake with rubber bands to the seat of my Schwinn bicycle and intentionally rode it over the bumpy roads throughout our housing tract, thus inventing the legendary Irish Baseball Glove Massage. Seldom in the annals of baseball lore have a boy and his glove been so close.

Step Two: Take the traumatized glove, now tenderized, and place the new baseball in its dark brown webbing in an attempt to create an *actual pocket*.

Step Three: Gently double the glove around the ball like an egg being folded over the cheese and mushrooms in an omelet.

Step Four: Use the nylon rope to bind the glove tightly, like a turkey being readied for the oven on Christmas Day. Suddenly, my senses were reeling. I didn't know if I wanted to play catch with my glove or *eat* the darn thing!

Step Five: No more Galloping Gourmet—back to reality. Now

we needed to place The Pancake, in all its prepared splendor, under a mattress. Not my dad's mattress. Not my sister's mattress. *My* mattress. No one had warned me that in order for my baseball glove to soar, I would first need to hatch it.

That first evening was the most difficult of many, many nights The Pancake and I spent together in nocturnal bliss. I kept thinking of the fairy tale where a common garden pea was secretly placed beneath the mattress of a young girl to determine if she was a real princess. If she could feel the pea through several mattresses, her royal bloodlines would be revealed. If not, she would be exposed as a fraud. Perhaps the same would be true with this leathery experiment. If I could feel the baseball within the glove beneath the mattress, then surely my place in baseball history was set and Joe DiMaggio would someday be asking for *my* autograph.

Turns out I had nothing to worry about. There was no disputing whether or not I could feel The Pancake. It was like sleeping on an armadillo, except that I think the armadillo would have been softer and more compliant with my needs. Weeks passed. Whenever I had a game to play, I would pull The Pancake out and untie it, expecting, hoping, dreaming that *this* was the day when my tragic caterpillar of a glove would transform into a monarch butterfly. Opening and closing. Opening and closing. Taking flight on the end of my hand as it lifted me a foot above the outfield fence to steal a home run and save the game for God and country. This, of course, never happened. I would temporarily free my glove, play the game, return home, then start the maddening process over again.

We gave The Pancake baseball-glove-oil therapy for about a year, but the patient never responded. Flat she was born and flat she remained until the day she went to baseball glove heaven.

But the experiment was not a total failure. Lo and behold—one day a pocket did form. It was on the underside of my mattress, a permanent reminder until the time I turned eighteen and moved out of my parents' house that once we had taken in an orphaned piece of leather, tried to rehabilitate it, and lost the battle.

Looking back, I realize that baseball glove oil was never going to answer the burning question of that time: "How do we turn this kid into the next Brooks Robinson?" Miracles of that magnitude don't often present themselves in small metal canisters retailing for a buck ninety-five.

Perhaps this was the wrong question. After all, how many players make the majors at any given time? Until baseball expands again to new cities, the answer is 750. There are more than six billion people in the world, and yet there are only 750 full-time slots open for the best of the best. Of those blessed few, how many will be enshrined in Cooperstown's Hall of Fame? One percent? Half a percent?

So what happens to the rest of us? How do we justify massive amounts of time spent apprenticing in a game we can never reasonably expect to master?

Well, maybe we start by measuring success not by the number of home runs, victories, or Gold Glove Awards we accumulate, but by the experience gained and the trials endured in the quest for these elusive grails. After all, there is no gold for the Olympic medal until it first passes through the refiner's fire that burns away every speck of dross. Indeed, the humiliation of owning The Pancake and allowing it to dangle from my right hand for a couple of seasons felt very much like this. Sometimes it seemed as if I were trapped in a large wrought-iron kettle while a raging inferno seared my body, pouring out spirit and soul ingot by ingot, Krugerrand by Krugerrand. And when there was nothing much left but a couple of fillings and some spare

We gave The Pancake baseball-glove-oil therapy for about a year, but the patient never responded.

change—well, this is when God does His best work.

While I was winding the rope around that ball and glove, attempting to shape a rudimentary tool to help me achieve whatever small goals and dreams I then understood—God was doing the same. He just didn't bother to mention that *I* was the tool He was shaping.

Through every mishap and embarrassment I suffered at the hands of The Pancake, God was winding His string of wisdom around my callow mind and heart, making me moldable, working character, perseverance, and, yes, even humility into the fresh young leather of my life. He was doing much more than helping me get ready for a Little League baseball game. He was preparing me, even then, for paths I could not imagine traveling and direction He would one day provide.

When the time came for God to call me up from the bench and onto His field of play, He had something finer for me than some ordinary oil. He poured out upon me the oil of His Holy Spirit, cascading like a waterfall over jagged rocks and ancient boulders, softening my heart, realigning my mind, anointing my ears to recognize His voice and my eyes to see His truth. This is the transformation He longs to perform. This is the gift He desires to share with each of us.

I had been looking for redemption through an oversized scrap of leather that betrayed me at every turn. It would be years before

> *While I was winding the rope around that ball and glove, attempting to shape a rudimentary tool to help me achieve whatever small goals and dreams I then understood—God was doing the same. He just didn't bother to mention that I was the tool He was shaping.*

I would look over to the third-base coach's box and realize God had been signaling to me His game plan all along.

Had I asked Him, would God have transformed my nightmarish mitt into the elusive glove of my secret dreams? I will never know. But radical change has always been one of God's signature plays. In His illustrious career He has touched the blind and given them sight. He has taken bent and broken lives and made them straight. So surely He could have taken something so miserably, perfectly straight like The Pancake and made it bent and broken.

He took water and changed it to wine. He takes sinners and wipes their slates clean. He took Saul—an angry, despicable murderer on the road to Damascus—broke him, humbled him, and molded him into a man named Paul, friend and apostle to Jesus, lover and preacher of the Word.

Oh, yeah…and he saved a wretch like me.

Pretty amazing.

And to think He did it all without even one drop of baseball glove oil.

Therefore, if anyone is in Christ,
he is a new creation;
the old has gone, the new has come!
—2 Corinthians 5:17

Finally, my father, who worked at the Library of Congress, smuggled me into the off-limits-to-the-public stacks. There in a musty corridor of deck 29 with GV862 overhead, my father said those fateful words, "Okay. Here is every book on baseball ever written. Don't go blind."

—Thomas Boswell

Third Inning

I Never Swang for My Father

Baseball was my father's game, although I'm not sure if he ever played it himself.

A pastime that particularly lent itself to sitting and watching, as opposed to active participation, baseball and my father were perfectly suited for each other. Baseball needed people to sit and watch for three hours, and, coincidentally, sitting-and-watching just happened to be one of my father's most finely honed skills. As an athlete, Dad made a wonderful spectator.

Now, my father could call this "slander" and have a lawyer on my porch in five minutes. But he won't. He knows better. He knows I am in possession of a short eight-millimeter film, made during the early sixties, of a father/son game in which he unwisely agreed to play. And he knows I won't hesitate to release this brutal evidence to *60 Minutes* should he press the matter.

My father swung the bat like he was swatting at flies—six or seven of the little suckers, it seemed, on every pitch. Of course, the apple didn't fall too far from the tree as far as my playing gifts were concerned. It seems in addition to the trademark red hair, freckles, and Richter Scale sneeze he bestowed upon me at birth, my father also encoded his hitting skills on my DNA.

In this archived clip, which has survived the years nicely

It seems in addition to the trademark red hair, freckles, and Richter Scale sneeze he bestowed upon me at birth, my father also encoded his hitting skills on my DNA.

despite some yellowing and occasional spotting, my father miraculously connected on a grounder to the shortstop. Even though there was no close-up, there is no mistaking the fear on his face nor the terror in his heart upon making contact. Clearly, hitting the ball fair was an event he had not even remotely considered when stepping up to take his hacks. And running the darn thing out was an eventuality for which he was entirely ill prepared.

Occasionally, I find myself watching this fluid snapshot from my youth, now that it has been transferred to video. Sometimes I will hit the Freeze option on my VCR and watch my dad, step by step, frame by frame, react with sheer horror at the thought of actually being thrown out by an eight-year-old.

As he finally crosses first base like a marathoner breaking tape, with relief dripping from every pore, triumphant in his masculinity, confident once more in his ability to dominate third graders, my father comes painfully close to taking out my diminutive teammate planted squarely on the bag. One 225-pound hip thrown in the wrong direction and the kid is a vegetable for life. Subliminal visions of a Mack truck plowing into a parked Corvette cause me to wince every time I return to this scene in my mind.

This ten-minute slice of home-movie footage is our family's Zapruder film. It is a living document and vivid testimony to the gene pool I fell into at birth and have been dog-paddling in ever since.

———————◆———————

One day when I was eight, my dad asked me if I wanted to join Little League. I didn't know what Little League was. It sounded like something for small people. At just under four feet, I was, it seemed, eminently qualified for this activity.

So my father purchased my first glove and signed me up. Turns out I was too little for Little League. So I was assigned to Pee Wee League.

Pee Wee League was where you went if you weren't big enough or good enough to make Little League. One assumes this was, indeed, the entry level for childhood baseball—that there was not something even more primitive in format like Infant League or Embryo Ball. But I never checked.

Today youngsters begin playing in something called T-ball. In T-ball the batter never has to face a pitcher, never has to worry about judging a ball or strike, never has to fear being hit on the helmet or arm. That's because there are no pitchers. T-ball is exactly what the name suggests: You place a baseball on a waist-high rubber tee, much as a golfer would to set up his first shot on each hole. Then you let the batter wreak holy havoc on the stationary sphere.

"Go ahead," you tell your son. "Beat this ball senseless and don't come back to the bench until you do!"

Strike out in T-ball and your mail will likely be forwarded to a military boarding school in Argentina.

The purpose of T-ball, it would seem, is to encourage self-esteem through the elimination of strikeouts.

What a shame.

In the early stages of my baseball career, I remember learning self-esteem through the hit I finally struck off a pretty good pitcher after making fifteen straight outs to start the season. I remember learning to like myself immensely after losing the first nine games by wide margins, then squeaking out a 10-9 victory in the tension-filled season finale.

But those were different times. Somehow, we relished those two-hour, two-inning 27-22 games with forty-six combined walks and just enough hits to count on the fingers of one hand. Call us crazy, but we kind of liked playing the game the way God intended—with real grass, pitchers who occasionally beaned batters, and wooden bats that—gasp!—actually broke or splintered from time to time.

Strike out in T-ball and your mail will likely be forwarded to a military boarding school in Argentina.

Aluminum, which in the seventies would be used to contain carbonated beverages and in the eighties to make lightweight baseball bats, was still, in the sixties, just a weapon in my mother's cookie-baking and food-wrapping arsenal. "Astro" was not yet a concept joined into unholy matrimony with the word "turf" but preceded, respectably, the word "physicist" and the not-quite-word "naut."

Of course, we also had not yet been "blessed" by the advent of the DH, or designated hitter. It would have been unthinkable for anyone on the team not to get his cuts like everybody else. In those days, we didn't even know what "designated" meant. Fortunately, we were young, impetuous kids whose literacy rates were rarely called into question on game day.

What we did understand, despite our limited vocabularies, was that we were supposed to take a designated swing at the designated ball and hope for a designated shot past the designated pitcher. On a designated run to the designated base you might take a designated glance at the designated play and hope the designated fielder who gloved your designated short-hop muffed his designated throw so the designated ump withheld his designated thumb that alone could catapult you back to your designated spot on the designated bench.

I played on a team called the Raineers. Other teams in the league had much more identifiable mascots. The Giants, the Red Sox, the Bears, the Mountaineers, and the Tigers all benefited from the undeniable fact that however well or badly they played, at least you knew *who* they were and *what* they represented.

Even the Mountaineers. Granted, one could make the argument that it wasn't much of a baseball nickname. They didn't exactly strike fear into the hearts of opponents who might, by other squads, be *squashed*, or *stomped*, or *mauled*. The best war cry a Mountaineer could likely muster was "I'll *climb* all over you!" Even so, the Mountaineers understood their genealogy.

But there was a simple question that fourteen little kids and their parents could not answer when taunted by their opponents:

"What the heck is a Raineer?"

None of us knew if it was animal, vegetable, or mineral. Maybe it was an entire population:

> *Documentary voice-over:* "The people of Raineria were an exciting anthropological find in the late 1800s...."

It might have been an exotic profession:

> *Television meteorologist:* "Raineers have been trying for months to provoke precipitation in the drought-ravaged land of Kenya but, so far, with little or no success...."

It wasn't fair. Even the Red Sox knew their roots, coming from good eastern argyle stock.

We were the orphans of Nicknamedom. And so our foes took to gleeful catcalls from the field as we batted: "Rain-*deers*, Rain-*deers*." They would ask us when Santa was coming, where the elves were, would Rudolph, with his nose so bright, be guiding our team around the bases tonight? And we, with heads bowed low, tried hiding the shame we felt as we took the derisive laughter into our little hearts. For we were the Raineers, the league's longest-running joke.

Years from now, someone in my hometown will be doing an investigative piece for the local paper, plowing through old county documents from the early 1960s. Like a latter-day Woodward or Bernstein, he will unwittingly stumble upon the truth about corruption at the lowest levels of organized baseball, unraveling a thread of backroom deals and graft that all point to a mysteriously named Pee Wee League team. There will be a bureaucrat at the center of

> *Even the Red Sox knew their roots, coming from good eastern argyle stock.*

the storm. He will have approved the use of a forsaken patch of land in the middle of nowhere in exchange for the naming rights to a single team. The man's name, bringing closure to the case, will be Ray Near.

I'm not sure, but I don't think Mom ever saw me play. If she did, I have forgotten. If, indeed, she sat in on one of my games, I have no doubt the memory is still with her.

My mother was born in Scotland and never really understood baseball. Mom wouldn't have known Jackie Robinson from Jackie

Gleason. All she knew was that her son was in love with a game that only loved him back a little. Yet that was good enough for her to wash and iron my dirty uniforms and help me decorate my bike with crepe paper for the Little League opening day parade each April.

Mom cooked my meals until I left home at eighteen, washed my clothes until a couple years after that, and sat up with me through more 102-degree temperatures than I can count. She saved her hard-earned baby-sitting money and sent her ten-year-old son to meet her parents, brother, and sister in Scotland during the summer of 1965.

So it's ironic that the thing I remember best about my mom—the one sacrifice of many that to this day stands out and touches me most—is the time she gave to the Little League snack bar.

For years I have wondered why Mom's snack-bar duty remains memorable through the passage of time and clings to my heart like barnacles to the hull of an ancient fishing boat. Maybe it's because all those other selfless acts—cooking, washing, nurturing, healing—seem like prerequisites on a mother's resume. You expect that from your mother. But snack-bar duty was above and beyond the normal call.

Mom wouldn't have known Jackie Robinson from Jackie Gleason. All she knew was that her son was in love with a game that only loved him back a little.

The work itself wasn't that tough. There were only two fountain drinks—Coca-Cola and orange soda. Actually there were three if you count the concoction that came from the mixing of both, affectionately dubbed a "Suicide" and generally ordered by the braver kids—the ones with constitutions stronger than that of the United States.

But you didn't exactly need to be a physicist to get the balance right. Fill the cup halfway up with Coke, then fill it the rest of the way with orange drink. Stirred, not shaken. That was the technique you were taught in snack-bar school, and it was sometimes potent enough to keep a kid out of class for a week.

The rest was just handing the correct candy bar or snack chip to the customer and making the right change. How do you get that wrong? No, the task was not equivalent to brain surgery, but the conditions were nearly as unappealing. I mean, who in their right minds would answer an ad like this:

Spend three- to four-hour shifts in cramped quarters doling out candy, popcorn, soft drinks, and Sno–Kones on blazing hot days to sometimes hurt and angry but always unappreciative Little League kids and their parents. No pay, no benefits, no air conditioning, and no chairs. Will likely take your son thirty years to appreciate the sacrifice you are making on his behalf. Apply within.

There can be only one explanation why a mother would place herself in sweatshop conditions with no immediate hope of reward. Or hazard pay. This was Mom's way of showing me, despite the fact there were no mother/son ball games, regardless of whether she could tell the difference between a Louisville Slugger and a cricket bat, that she wanted to support this strange activity that had suddenly grabbed my heart and slid safely into my soul. I wish I had understood this earlier, but I suppose this is the sort of gesture one can only appreciate with time, distance, and becoming a parent yourself.

◆

My father, on the other hand, recognized his civic duty and enlisted before a draft became necessary. Armed with amply padded, strategically placed layers of natural cushioning, patiently engineered through years of dedicated *Bonanza* and *Ed Sullivan* viewing, Dad had a different take on volunteerism. Although he never again ventured onto the field for a hard dose of competitive reality, my dad, with little fanfare, made a selfless commitment to sit in the stands and watch me play in most of my games.

Unfortunately, there were no stands for the Pee Wee field.

In truth, there was very little field.

We lived in a brand-new community, a suburb of California's state capital called Foothill Farms. However, the Sacramento County Parks and Recreation Department hadn't really made a strong commitment to us yet. Abandoned to our own devices, we were sort of the Donner Party of start-up baseball leagues. I guess Parks and Recreation was just waiting to see if we lasted a couple winters before sinking any serious tax money into a real park for our recreation.

Yes, there was a chicken-wire backstop no more than twelve feet across. But the fenceless outfield consisted entirely of dry weeds and bramble. The infield was bare and generally clear of tumbleweeds, which was one positive, for we were still learning to field ground balls, and anything else moving on the infield would have been a dangerous distraction.

The pitcher's mound was one in name only, owing to its utter lack of elevation. The heart of the mound showcased a foot-long white strip—kind of a poor man's pitching rubber—fashioned from a Tupperware lid some mother had donated to the cause.

This rubber not only legitimized the vast prairie from which youthful hurlers earned their keep in Pee Wees, but served an important community function as well. Occasionally gas pockets would collect underground. When this happened, the Board of Supervisors were called, environmental studies commissioned, and, eventually, a county safety engineer would be dispatched to "burp" our mound for a few minutes until the situation was well in hand.

Surely there were worse playing conditions somewhere in the world—say, Antarctica. But there was not one blade of grass within a square mile of our desolate outpost that, for whatever reason, had been mysteriously labeled "Lot D."

Throughout the country, families assembled for time-honored battles on lush green acres of sod, these fields and parks named after famous baseball players and deceased—or wealthy—community leaders. We played all our games on Lot D, which sounded more like a cryptic moniker the CIA would give a top-secret alien landing site than a place you cherished, where you grew up learning the timeless game of our fathers.

Since there were no stands, no bleachers, parents brought their own folding lawn chairs and littered the first- and third-base areas with them. Occasionally, one of the chairs would collapse, trapping a hapless adult in a merciless web of nylon and aluminum until the Fire Department could be called and the Jaws of Life employed.

A rich, generous slice of the American pie, the Foothill Farms Little League, as a pastoral landscape, lay somewhere between the works of Norman Rockwell and Salvador Dali. *Field of Dreams* meets *Death Valley Days*.

Whether I was in the outfield, the on-deck circle, or even riding the pine simply busting for a chance to get in the game, I was always keenly aware of Dad's presence. He didn't have to do anything special. He wasn't much for yelling his encouragement. For some reason the ballpark was a place he was usually subdued. Through a bustle of noise and excitement I could sometimes make out his subtle monotone, urging me on to greatness: "OK, Mike. Come on now." He would clap softly a couple times for emphasis.

Other parents got excited. Other parents raised their voices. Other parents used *adjectives*. "OK, Mike. Come on now" was about as worked up as my dad could get at a baseball game.

But he really *meant* it.

Some fathers must have seen themselves as extensions of their sons' gifts and abilities, because they maintained an insufferable vocal presence—boasting to other parents, shouting play-ing instructions, berating the umpire—whether their kids were batting or not. It was as if the game and boy existed to feed their bottomless egos. I grew to despise these men and pitied their sons, the seemingly confident kids at practice who shriveled to emotional wads of gum after being chewed up and spit out by these bullies in their postgame tirades.

The contests were supposed to be fun. Maybe along the way we even learned a lesson or two about sportsmanship, teamwork, discipline. My dad must have understood all this, because he pretty much left me alone to play the game. He did his best not to interfere.

He wasn't like Robert Young or Andy Griffith, those sixties TV dads dispensing sage advice in thirty-minute gulps. How could he have been? When my father was just four years old, he lost his mother to cancer. His father, having no idea what to do with a boy that young, farmed him out to a series of friends and relatives. During many of my father's formative years, he had no primary male role model in his life. None, at least, who would call him son.

Several years later, my grandfather remarried and reclaimed his offspring. Unfortunately, this turned out to be more like a pawn-shop transaction than a joyful reunion. Buried in his work at the Southern Pacific Railroad, and perhaps in residual grief, my grand-father had little room in his heart for my father. There was duty toward a boy he barely knew—and that was about it.

Often my dad would find his father in the garage, working on a home improvement project or the family car. When Dad asked, "Can I help?" my grandfather inevitably chased him off. "What can *you* do?" he would sneer, returning to his work. This was pretty much the environment in which my dad grew up. All in all, not a particularly nurturing atmosphere.

Little wonder, then, that parenting a son and two daughters was far from natural for him. He was awkward with us, but not altogether distant. During Lawrence Welk's Saturday-night champagne music he might suddenly become Fred Astaire as my sisters Patricia and Kathleen glided dreamily across the living room rug on the tops of his worn brown slippers.

Dad was uncomfortable with tender emotional displays. How could it have been any different? In a sense, he was a carpenter without his own set of tools. Looking to build his own family, he had been given no foundation for the task and had never seen a working blueprint.

He played his part the way it had been scripted, like his father and grandfather before him. The Irish are nothing if not steeped in tradition. Mustering inner strength, he struggled for independence from his legacy. When he stepped out from the long shadow his own father cast, fleshing out the role of dad with more mercy and love than he had ever known, I believe he was finally able to find some level of ease walking in his own shoes.

Dad was uncomfortable with tender emotional displays. How could it have been any different? In a sense, he was a carpenter without his own set of tools. Looking to build his own family, he had been given no foundation for the task and had never seen a working blueprint.

When I needed advice, he was rarely verbose. Dad almost always let the lesson come to me. But that was all right. Some of the best teachers I have ever encountered were the ones who gave me just enough information, just enough technique—then stood back and allowed me to grow.

My father was not the most brilliant man in the world. He had his faults, his weaknesses, and the legendary Irish temper that he generously passed on to his only son. Yet he had an excellent sense of when to be there for me—and when to get out of the way. He never pushed me into activities I disliked. He simply spread out the options and let me choose.

Today, being a father myself, I realize this is what a dad does. Guidance, along with a little thing called "provision," is his entire job. He is a rudder for the boat. He helps you steer clear of boulders in the stream. But if the child is ever going to navigate the waters of life, there comes a time when he has to row the boat himself. Too many fathers don't want to hand over the oars—or do so far too late.

◆

I am fortunate. I don't have many regrets concerning my playing days. The few I have are documented herein. Good or bad, I played the game as well as I knew how. I am a better man today for the lessons I have learned between the lines—and outside them as well.

But if I could stow away on Mr. Peabody's Way-Back Machine and travel across time, if I had a chance through some miracle of technology or theology to change one element of my game, it would be this: I wish I had played a little less selfishly.

Oh, I understood the concept of *team* just fine. I loved my teammates and did my best to integrate whatever talent God gave me toward the worthwhile ends of teamwork and camaraderie.

But when a fly ball was hit my way or I stood in the batter's box awaiting the first pitch, I remember thinking I was the center of everything. At this moment the sun rose and set on me. The planets aligned on my whim. Humanity held its collective breath while I took my turn.

Perhaps this was because I was born on the middle day of one of the middle months in the middle of the twentieth century in the capital city of the most glamorous state in the most powerful country on the most important planet in the most breathtaking solar system in our known galaxy. Or perhaps I suffered from delusions of grandeur. But life just *seemed* to revolve around me.

And never more so than when my dad was watching me play. I remember thinking—like any kid, I suppose—*I need to get a hit. I want to make my dad proud of me*. Now, there is nothing inherently abnormal about that sentiment. The equation is fairly universal:

Getting on base = Daddy loves me.

But what if you ground out? Does this mean Daddy no longer loves you? Sadly, in some cases, it does. But love—real love, true love, the pure and selfless kind we find alive and breathing in the way Jesus walked it out in the New Testament—is not conditioned on any specific outcome.

> *I remember thinking—like any kid, I suppose*—I need to get a hit. I want to make my dad proud of me.

When I tied my father's approval to feats of athleticism, I exhibited selfishness. I wanted to do well so he could be proud of me, so he could turn to the other dads and brag on his son, so he could bask in *my* reflected glory. When I took my cuts, I swung the bat to add prestige to *my* name—to magnify *my* reputation.

Why wasn't I driven toward that same greatness for my *father's* glory, to magnify *his* name? Maybe the other dads would have slapped him on the back or bought him a hot dog because of what his son had done for the team.

Or better yet, why didn't I shine the spotlight of favor on my father—my mother too—every time it shone on me…just because I loved them?

Because I was eight or ten or twelve or seventeen. Because it has taken me a long time to wrap my mind around this basic concept: "Honor thy father and thy mother."

◆

I rewind the film and watch it with fresh eyes. I see a man, middle-aged, risking humiliation before his peers because he loves his son and wants to make him proud. He's swinging the bat. He's made contact. He's running. He's trying. He's determined. He's safe. He's exhilarated. He's avoided a manslaughter charge. He's proud. He's breathless. And maybe, for an instant, he feels ten years old again and scans the crowd, hoping *his* father has come to share this moment—to bask in the glow of a son's first hit.

How can I tell the man who put the first baseball in my hand...who guided my bicycle down the street the day he removed its training wheels...who sat cross-legged on the floor with me in full headdress at meetings of Y-Indian Guides...how do I tell him, without sounding corny or condescending, what I know with absolute certainty?

Oh, yes...He was there, Dad.

The One who created you for this world and loved you before you were born...who tended your wounded heart and broken dreams as you were kicked around from home to home. He was there, watching just beyond sight.

Your Father was there.

*The Lord himself goes before you
and will be with you; he will never
leave you nor forsake you. Do not be
afraid; do not be discouraged.*
—Deuteronomy 31:8

Fourth Inning

No Crying in Baseball

Had the pitcher noticed my right foot twitching nervously on the bag, he would have easily surmised my criminal intent. Sweat soaked the upper portion of my uniform, the back of which proclaimed the virtues of Brown's Hardware Store. Two batters had come and gone, fastball victims now reposing in the statistical morgue of the official scorekeeper. But still I remained anchored after my leadoff single.

So long had I been on first base, it had become a second home to me. I was getting mail there now. Social security checks would be arriving soon. Yet there was no sign from Mr. Barclay in the third-base coach's box. No signal flare. No buried newspaper classified whispering that a dash to freedom was imminent. Second base, the promised land, was sixty feet away, but I may as well have been standing on Alcatraz.

Maybe it was the heat. It must have been ninety-five degrees that day, and the sweltering valley sun surely extracted all reason from my brain. Perhaps it was the boredom. A fellow can go stir-crazy waiting around for a jailbreak. It might have been a rare polar event, as the magnetic pull between me and that square-shaped flour sack could not have been stronger. Does it really matter why? Looking back, I see I really had no choice. I was as helpless as a sailor succumbing to the call of the Sirens.

Second base, the promised land, was sixty feet away, but I may as well have been standing on Alcatraz.

History will record that on the first pitch to the inning's fourth batter, as the baseball hit the center of the catcher's glove, the sound of horse-hide kissing cowhide conspired to simulate a starter's pistol. At least this is how I remember it. I do know it was an electrifying sound that startled me into action. Never mind I had gotten a late jump. Never mind I had no plan. I bolted for my destination like a turkey being chased on Thanksgiving.

Surely the well-known fact that I was the league's slowest runner would only shock and fluster the catcher into stupefying inaction. Surely as my quest was noble and my heart was true, the ball would sail over the covering shortstop's reach into center field. Surely I had not counted on the quick release or the straight throw that was waiting for me as I reached the midway point of my incredible journey.

My eyes grew wide. I had not considered this possibility. I was about to feel the sting of baseball mortality. In one game-time instant I experienced the entire spectrum of Dr. Kubler-Ross's five stages of death: Denial, Anger, Bargaining, Depression, and finally, Acceptance. As I strolled into second with the force of a train half an hour after the coal is depleted, I felt a dysfunctional obligation to slide, though it was merely a formality. Denial had decided to step back into the box and take some extra cuts. Quitting, even when clearly the wisest course of action, is not a concept I have ever embraced graciously.

To my discredit and lasting embarrassment, I tried a last-minute trick slide, which led me to dance out of the basepath and into shallow center field where, from my opponent's flank, I then threw my body at the base in a final, desperate, twisted flailing lunge that could very well have inspired spectators to throw a telethon on my behalf.

As I strolled into second with the force of a train half an hour after the coal is depleted, I felt a dysfunctional obligation to slide, though it was merely a formality.

The umpire was generous. He could have made one of those huge arm-motion calls that looks like a pitcher winding up and throwing the ball straight into the ground with raw, brutal force. For indeed, I had been shot down from Austin to Dallas and deserved as much. Instead, he looked at me with compassion, clenched his meaty fist gently, and muttered, "Yer out, son."

The shame of it all. Oh, the humanity! I lay on my back wondering *What should I do now?* If a game show were somehow magically to have broken out right there on the diamond, the final *Jeopardy* question would have been, "What is get up, dust yourself off, and look as good as you can jogging back to the dugout?" Instead, I panicked and chose a regrettable course.

I started crying.

That's right. The faucet was opened and the waterworks flowed. I tried to stop. The dirt was puddling up around second base. I knew this wasn't good. I knew the coach would come out on the field looking for an ankle injury. I knew I would be ribbed mercilessly by the players of both teams the next day at school. Eventually, all these came to pass. But I couldn't help myself. I had been found guilty of hubris and was sentenced to the spectacle of public humiliation. If tears could have melted me as the bucket of water did Margaret Hamilton in *The Wizard of Oz*, I would have been grateful for the escape.

Instead, I was led off the field by Mr. Barclay, bawling my eyes out. But hey, I was ten years old that day. Nobody had ever *explicitly* warned me about the taboo I had broken, nor the cardinal rule I would be encouraged to follow the rest of my days. We didn't even know the specific words, but I and about a billion other testosterone-laden boys had this overtly macho precept engraved on our hearts the day we were born. Even so, it took thirty years before someone spoke an amazing phrase that opened our ears to the emotional holocaust we young citizens of baseball had been subject to since the first time we picked up a ball and bat.

It came, as so many universal moments do, in the movies. The film was *A League of Their Own*, the true story of the women's baseball league that entertained Americans during World War II. In one scene, a young woman had just made an egregious fielding error, throwing the ball to the wrong base. Approaching the dugout after the inning, her manager, played by Tom Hanks, gave her a scathing earful of advice on the merits of hitting the cut-off man, er, woman. In an instant, she was reduced to tears. Hanks was stunned. He, a veteran manager and grizzled former major leaguer, had, apparently, never witnessed such an event on a ball field.

"Are you *crying?*" he inquired, dumbfounded. "There's no *crying*. There's no crying in *baseball!*"

And there it was. As boys, we had been chastened by fathers, coaches, teachers—anyone in authority—that we were young men and needed to reign in our feelings. Bite the bullet. Tough it out. Stiff upper lip. The Four Seasons' sixties hit "Big Girls Don't Cry" seems to have had virtually no impact on the young women of our day, but "Walk Like a Man" was surely the emotional anthem for a generation of male baby boomers.

There's no crying in baseball?

Sez who? Tom Hanks? My dad? Mr. Barclay? I want to know. Who invented this line of propaganda? Ever since I first set foot on a baseball diamond—most certainly forever after—as I follow the game through radio, television, newspaper, and countless biographies and historical accounts, I am struck time and time again by how closely baseball parallels our daily lives.

The truth is that baseball not only brings out but encourages the humanity in us. The game is a festival of emotional excess. When so much in life tells us to keep our feelings close to the vest, baseball has always been a signed permission slip to let go of whatever needs releasing. You name it, baseball invites it. For better or for worse, joy, pity, anger, regret, envy, jubilation, despair, euphoria, amazement, hatred, respect, laughter—these are all elements that are played out on the field and in the stands, inning after inning, game after game, season after season.

And crying.

But don't take my word for it. Who can forget "the Iron Horse," Lou Gehrig, addressing sixty-two thousand fans on Lou Gehrig Appreciation Day, July 4, 1939? Gehrig, one of the true greats in Yankee history, had been diagnosed with ALS (later informally designated as "Lou Gehrig's Disease"), which had cut short his brilliant career. This was his farewell to the fans, his teammates, and the game he so dearly loved. He could have filled Yankee Stadium with mounds of

> *Baseball not only brings out, but encourages, the humanity in us. The game is a festival of emotional excess.*

self-pity. After what he'd been through, he was entitled. Instead, he sealed his legend with these simple words:

"Fans, for the past two weeks you have been reading about a bad break I got. Yet today I consider myself the luckiest man on the face of the earth."

The *luckiest* man? Did we hear that right? Could we roll tape and check that again, please? Was this man, whose muscles were betraying him, who soon would lose all mobility and ability to speak, swallow, and, eventually breathe—was this man looking into a sea of humanity and telling us he was *fortunate* to find himself in this circumstance?

I wasn't alive in 1939. But I've seen the film footage and heard the speech on an old record I used to own. If you've only seen Gary Cooper's version of this moment in *Pride of the Yankees*, I'm here to say, "You ain't seen nothin'." Because nothing can replace the impact of that moment with Lou Gehrig courageously sharing his heart with the masses in Yankee Stadium. By all press accounts, the tears flowed freely as those present showered their ailing hero with love from their hearts and their eyes.

And while we're on the subject, I simply can't watch *Field of Dreams* without completely losing it. I've seen it five—maybe six—times. And whenever Kevin Costner's character, Ray, asks the youthful image of his long-deceased father, this man against whom he's held a lifetime of grudges and anger, if he wants to play catch—well, I turn into a blubbering idiot. It doesn't matter how many times I've seen it. Doesn't matter that I know what's coming. When Ray's dad answers solemnly, "I'd like that," I'm worthless for the next two hours.

No crying in baseball? Explain that to the young boy who wept for Dodger catcher Roy Campanella when he lost his career and the use of his legs after a late-night car accident just before the Brooklyn team moved to Los Angeles. Or to *that* boy's son upon learning of Thurman Munson's tragic death after crashing the small instructional plane he was piloting. Or to *that* boy's son who exulted as he witnessed unbreakable records being shattered by his heroes Cal Ripken Jr. and Mark McGwire in the late nineties. Or to *that* boy's son who will one day grieve as his beloved team falls one game short of winning it all on the season's final day.

A popular theory today holds that we oozed out of the sludge and muck and somehow evolved from slugs and apes into these incredible bodies we now possess.

The Bible tells us that God made man in His own image. I believe this is true. If I'm wrong, then I'm a monkey's uncle. But I see too much evidence of God's perfect planning to believe otherwise. God is the ultimate engineer. He designed us in minute, perfect detail. There were no accidents in the design—not even with those who appear, in our limited vision, to have been produced imperfectly.

Tears are an integral piece of that blueprint. They are part of the plumbing God installed with the foundation. Like a good rain cleansing the air of impurities, a good cry is often cathartic and leaves mind, body, and spirit feeling cleansed and refreshed, renewed and restored.

One final example.

Philip Roth attained the goal of every author who dreams of one day writing the great American novel in his 1973 book, *The Great American Novel*. The story revolves around a mythical third baseball entity, the Patriot League, formed to compete with the American and National Leagues. My favorite character, Ulysses S. Fairsmith, is an eighty-year-old gentleman who manages his team from the comfort of his rocking chair in the corner of the dugout. He never wears the team uniform as other managers do, preferring his white shirt, silk bow tie, white linen suit, and Panama hat. He has never set foot in a ballpark on Sunday, owing to a promise he made to his mother. He is, in short, a throwback to a simpler time and place.

The most memorable characteristic of this gentle man was the way he would take the ball from a pitcher whom he was relieving of duty. It didn't matter if a hurler had pitched eight shutout innings or just walked six batters in a row. He would always have the same kind words: "Thank you very much for the effort. I'm deeply grateful to you." I have read this wonderful story many times, and those words never fail to bring tears to my eyes. In all my years of working I have never had a boss like this. And somewhere, deep down, I yearn for one who would appreciate my efforts more fully. Don't we all?

I once worked for a man who warned me the day I was hired that he would never pay me a compliment, even if I was doing a good job. When I asked him why, he told me he had once commended one of his workers, it went to his head, and the clerk quit because he realized he was too good for that place. I quit after eleven months because this man didn't have enough money to compensate me for the kindness that he never gave.

Now, whenever I read Mr. Fairsmith's words (and I have reread them often), I think of the kind of employer I'd want to be. I think of the deep-seated desire for approval in my life. And I realize Mr. Fairsmith represents something more to me. He says, "Thank you very much for the effort. I'm deeply grateful to you." But I hear another voice, an even gentler one whispering, "Well done…well done, good and faithful servant." And I realize there is longing in my heart I have not yet begun to understand. I think of a day when there will be no more yearning, no more suffering, no more need for tears. There is wonderful peace in this.

Then I remember a ten-year-old boy in a baseball uniform. Maybe he wasn't really looking for that extra base. Maybe his mind was really on home: the warmth, the safety, the reward he wanted so badly—his father's approval—and he just couldn't wait to get there. Maybe he just wanted someone to say, "Well done…well done, good and faithful Little Leaguer."

I think about him lying there in the dust, and I want to go back and tell him everything will be OK—that one day he *will* be safe at home—there will be no more sadness, no more embarrassing moments—and I know the way, if only he will follow. But the years are a one-way mirror. I can see him, yet he cannot communicate with me. So he's going to have to learn his lessons through trials of fire.

I can see him wiping the dirt from his uniform, preparing for that looooonnng walk back to the dugout. There is so much life, so much joy, so many difficulties before him. And despite all the well-intentioned advice and sound training I have received through the years, when I picture him walking back from second base with that affected limp, I cry.

> *For the Lamb at the center of the*
> *throne will be their shepherd;*
> *he will lead them to the springs of*
> *living water.*
> *And God will wipe away every tear*
> *from their eyes.*
> —*Revelation 7:17*

*A life isn't significant except
for its impact on other lives.*

—Jackie Robinson

*There is one word in America that says it all
and that word is "You never know."*

—Joaquin Andujar

Fifth Inning

A Tale of Two Coaches

It was *the best of times, it was the worst of times. It was a time-less time, sealed in a capsule, devoid of time; a time for reflection, as time marched on, for time hangs heavy when it's time for change.*

Once upon a time before time was money, as it scurried about obsessively healing all wounds and making sure it was air-borne while everyone was having fun, a time card was slipped, a time clock punched, and the time-honored concept of time and a half was granted a well-deserved timeout.

Given time off for good behavior and knowing full well that, generally, time waits for no man…time, uncharacteristically, stood still and waited as I pondered the uncertain future before me….

I was was finally graduating from Pee Wee to Little League, having completed the grueling, transitional prerequisite, which mostly entailed arriving at age nine still breathing.

Young, naïve, feeling terribly conflicted, I stood at the precipice of tomorrow and peered off into the abyss. Behind me stretched the chain link fence of history. There was simply no returning without a time machine and a good set of wire cutters.

Before me lay endless possibilities. But sometimes decisions can be daunting when your biggest choice to date has been between Vanilla and Rocky Road.

Holding a baseball glove in one hand and a sack lunch containing a Velveeta and Spam sandwich in the other, I stood before eternity and weighed my options.

On one hand, the obvious perks: Advancement. Prestige. Bleachers for the spectators. Fields with actual grass. Bubble gum on demand.

On the other hand, the deep concerns: Leaving the warmth and security of the baseball womb. Faster pitching. Higher parental expectations. Will anyone notice if I ditch this sandwich into the abyss?

Behind me stretched the chain link fence of history. There was simply no returning without a time machine and a good set of wire cutters.

I can't speak for the other kids. That would make me a ventriloquist. But I was more than a bit nervous entering my new environs. I felt like an East German citizen crossing the border to the West. I was certain some stern Little League official would stop me just short of the chalk on the third-base line and check my papers. Realizing I was an imposter, he would set loose the dogs and reward my fraudulent run for baseball freedom with machine-gun spray. Or, at least, hysterical laughter.

Before long, I began to realize how foolish this notion had

been. In the new season, once I took the logical step up to The Bigs, I began to feel almost grown up. Having slipped into the bright yellow cap and white flannel uniform of the Foothill Farms Little League Cubs, I surveyed the sprawling green diamond where I would spend the next three years of my fledgling baseball life.

Amazingly, no one bothered to verify whether or not I held credentials for this lofty new level of play. Before long my youthful trepidation succumbed to the confident swagger of one who finally understands he belongs. I say "swagger" because I brought to my new elevation a piece of information so eye-opening and, dare I say, revolutionary in its scope that scores of books and master's theses have since been written on the subject. That I was never credited with this quantum leap in physics grieves me not. Some men are born to greatness…others have it wrenched from their tiny little fists.

Somewhere in the middle of my first season in Pee Wees, I had learned that if you take the bat off your shoulder and use it to lunge at a baseball the pitcher has recently released, your chances of hitting that ball skyrocket exponentially.

I'm really not sure the precise moment the muse tapped me on the helmet with her Popsicle-stick-sized bat and drilled this bit of wisdom into me. I think it may have been on the downbeat of that age-old chorus the opposition delighted in sharing with me each time I stepped up to the plate:

"HEY…batta, batta, batta, batta…SWING!"

Yes, that was definitely the moment of epiphany. This eloquent mantra penetrated my still-tender head and navigated the depths of my subconscious, preparing fertile ground for this prime directive:

"SWING…batta, batta, batta, batta…Suh-WING!"

I became wonderfully adept at following the opposing fielders' advice during my first season with the Cubs. Although my strike-outs stayed at their previous level and my walks were placed by the Sierra Club on the endangered species list, I am proud to say that my incidences of grounding out to the catcher went through the roof!

And despite the fact that my batting average was languishing somewhere below the parental-approval rating the Beatles enjoyed in a 1964 Gallup poll, I was a swinging fool having the time of my life out there on God's lush green field.

Then somewhere in the middle of that first season as a Cub, something strange, and eerie, and wonderfully mysterious occurred. I got the rest of it. The lost fragment of the equation. The Loch Ness monster beached. The "Who shot J. R.?" of base-ball methodology.

Previously, in Pee Wees, my understanding of the batter's mission statement had always been:

Pitched ball + Swung bat = Strikeout

But experience was a noble teacher. Somehow I had stumbled upon the missing link to health, happiness, and free sodas after the game:

Pitched ball + Swung bat + Eyes open = Youneverknow

There were also several other revelations that season involving square roots, decimals, and long division, but suffice to say that hitting the ball squarely was not nearly the problem it had been before. My batting average was hovering around .400. My confidence was soaring. Suddenly, my fielding improved and I was moved from the graveyard of right field to second base, a veritable hotbed of activity.

You have to understand what an honor this was. I was a lefty.

There are about as many left-handed second basemen in baseball history as men who have walked on the moon. The reasons? Well, a glove on the right hand is great when going up the middle to field a ball. But it leaves the fielder vulnerable to the ball hit to the huge area between the first and second basemen. To field a ball in that gap the second sacker must either reach awkwardly across his body for the grab or compensate by moving farther out of his territory than may be wise.

Then there is the double play. With a runner on first, the second baseman must be able to receive the throw on his bag, make the essential pivot, and throw to first in time to nab the batter. This is a ballerina-like task under the best of circumstances. Being a southpaw is hardly ever the best of circumstances.

A lefty must take that throw moving away from first, touch the bag, leap in the air off-balance, and swivel three-quarters to face first and release a ball that, considering physical laws, will likely have very little speed on it, even if he has a cannon for an arm.

In essence, my coach, Mr. Barclay, was saying to me, "I trust you, son." That's all anyone ever needs to hear, isn't it? He may as well have given me the keys to his car and the hand of his daughter. His faith in me meant more than I could ever tell him.

Barclay was a tall, slender man who wore some sort of hat most of the time—owing, as I recall, to a hairline that was receding like wildfire. At the time he seemed ancient. But considering that his son Sean was a teammate around my age, he probably wasn't much more than thirty-five.

> *In essence, my coach, Mr. Barclay, was saying to me, "I trust you, son."*

He was serious and no-nonsense during practice. He possessed a strong voice and sharp tongue, yet was never vulgar in our presence. With other men I am sure he was capable of coarseness.

No doubt the army missed out on a great drill sergeant. Even so, with a ball and a fungo bat in his hands, he never forgot that he was in the company of boys.

The man was no saint. From time to time he exhibited traces of temper. But, like a ball hit to center field, he was always fair. He would give you chance after chance after chance if he saw you were trying, no matter how miserable the results. He hated laziness, though, and would sit his best player at game time if the kid gave less than his abilities allowed.

He may as well have given me the keys to his car and the hand of his daughter.

Winning was not overly stressed. Still, our string of second-place finishes is a testament to our fearless leader—a man whose lessons on both sides of the foul line continue to reside in the minds and hearts of those whose job is now to pass the wisdom along to a new generation of nine- to twelve-year-olds swimming upstream.

I played three years for Mr. Barclay's Cubs. I would have played on his team forever, but Little League has a mandatory retirement age that precludes guys who shave, vote, or use Poli-Grip.

Little League graduated me at twelve and one year later handed a teenager over to Babe Ruth Baseball. In those three years I had continually grown into a good, competent (if unspectacular) player.

I was in junior high now, coming off my best season. I was primed to make the jump to the next level, where the pitches would be thrown harder and some of them, rumor had it, would even bend before they reached the plate. Today millions of men, major leaguers at heart, are employed in industries not entirely of their own choosing. Most can trace their entry to these gray, grassless fields to the introduction of the curve ball in their lives.

The boys in this league were beginning to look like small men. We had strange new hair sprouting from our armpits and strange new odors emanating from the same vicinity.

I entered Babe Ruth ball brimming with confidence. I was a seventh grader on the verge of manhood and didn't care who knew it. But the self-assurance would be short-lived.

For the fourth consecutive year I would be playing on a team named "Cubs." What are the odds? Although I hoped to someday become a "Bear" or a "Grizzly"—even a "Panda" would be a step in the right direction—the big red "C" on my yellow felt hat had been lucky the past three years, and I supposed I could carry the baby bears' banner a little longer. After all, this was to be my breakout campaign.

Yet a man was about to enter my life who would change all that.

Ron Tucker was a colleague of my father's at their place of employment. As I recall, my placement on his Babe Ruth team came as some sort of favor to my dad. Whatever my dad's reciprocation—free lunch, trading days off, a stick of gum—the price would prove entirely too high.

Coach Tucker was not only a perfectionist but an excellent baseball strategist. On our first day of practice, he handed each of us a mimeographed playbook for defensive alignments showing us what to do and when to do it. The playbook laid out just about every possible circumstance a fielder could face in any given game.

I played three years for Mr. Barclay's Cubs. I would have played on his team forever, but Little League has a mandatory retirement age that precludes guys who shave, vote, or use Poli-Grip.

For instance, if the ball were hit down the right-field line with no runner on base, the second baseman would find the prescribed spot in shallow right, creating a straight line between where the outfielder would pick up the ball and second base. If the right fielder had enough gas on the ball to have a chance of nailing the sliding runner, the second baseman would let the ball go through. But if the fielder had a weak arm, as did most right fielders I had ever met, the second baseman would act as a cutoff man and relay the throw to the shortstop covering second. The pitcher would be backing up third base in case an error were made or the hit turned into a triple.

A place for every player and every player in his place. It was a good system that taught us advanced defensive techniques our Little League coaches had not.

Mr. Tucker held practices before the season started. It was determined I would play right field, as the coach already had all the left-handed second basemen he could use. Imagine that—just thirteen years old and already I was a victim of downsizing.

I had some early difficulties tracking fly balls hit to me, as it had been two years since I had patrolled any outfield. In Pee Wees and Little League, we had been *requested*, but not *expected*, to actually catch long fly balls. We, of the clueless outfield brethren, merely followed the errant spheres until they stopped rolling, briskly running them back to the infield in the same way you would return a Dr. Pepper bottle to the corner grocery.

I was also having trouble during batting practice picking up the ball, with its newfound curves, unexpected drops, and increased velocity. I knew I could catch up to the team's needs and the coach's demands. I just needed a little more practice. A little more patience. A little more time.

Soon Mr. Tucker had seen enough of his players to make iron-clad appraisals of us. And the judgments, however exact or premature, stuck like metal shavings in a magnet factory.

We were, I believe, systematically herded into two classes. Group A: The first string. The studs. The starters. Those troops who could help this general take enough battles to win him the war. Group B: Everyone else. The scrubs. The half-talents. The hangers-on. Those kids who should have retired after Little League.

Coach Tucker had little patience for the handful of Bs he had been saddled with. Most of us were rotated in and out of right field, batted ninth, and played the absolute minimum number of innings permitted by league regulations. Gone were the days of "atta-boys" and "don't-worry-about-its."

I received precious little nurturing or encouragement in my time under this coach, but I could absolutely count on a butt-chewing or a long, slow glare if I'd blown a play or been a step slow in getting to a ball.

It would have been one thing if he was evenhanded in his cold manner. But it was a different tale entirely if you were one of his stars. Coach Tucker buddied up to the guys who made strong contributions. He slapped them on the back, told them crude jokes as if they were men, and treated the rest as though we ought to run home to Mommy for cookies and milk. He gave these seventh and eighth graders chewing tobacco during games and allowed them to call him by his first name.

I had no interest in these extracurricular activities that seemed to bond the first-string boys to their coach. Still, the emptiness is palpable when your nose is pressed against the glass and you want nothing more than to belong. A leper outside the gates, relegated to his little colony at the end of the bench, I learned firsthand the shame of

We were, I believe, systematically herded into two classes. Group A: The first string. The studs. The starters. Those troops who could help this general take enough battles to win him the war. Group B: Everyone else. The scrubs. The half-talents. The hangers-on. Those kids who should have retired after Little League.

separation. I vowed I would never again exclude someone from joining in just because their beauty may not be obvious or their talent less than apparent. Alas, experience has shown me that this is the hardest promise in the world to keep.

Babe Ruth ball, like Congress, offered a two-year stint that, like it or not, was to be served on the same team. There were no trades or new drafts of established players. Quitting appeared to be the only way off a Babe Ruth team. I wasn't about to give my coach that satisfaction.

To me Mr. Tucker had been more like a warden than a baseball coach. I served my time and moved on.

I vowed I would never again exclude someone from joining in just because their beauty may not be obvious or their talent less than apparent. Alas, experience has shown me that this is the hardest promise in the world to keep.

But I was never the same player again. I lost two years of precious development and was never again a first-stringer. My confidence had been squashed, yet no one could touch my love for the game.

For the next couple of seasons, my freshman and sophomore years in high school, I shied away from playing and dedicated my energies to being manager of the Foothill High School varsity baseball team. "Manager" was just a glorified way of labeling the jobs of batboy and water-boy. But I was content to be near the game in just about any capacity. And the position brought a certain amount of status, as I was hanging out with guys two and three years older who regularly got their names in the *Sacramento Bee*. I did my job well and was treated with respect by the coach and players. I'm sure the guys must have wondered why anyone would endure the rigors of servitude with little or no glory attached. There was no way for them to see, or for me to understand at the time, that I was giving a wound time to heal.

For two summers I signed on to be manager of the McClellan Air Force Base American Legion team. Again, these were high school juniors and seniors playing in one of the most respected amateur baseball programs in the country. My duties were similar to those I had known. Serve water, pick up bats, hit fungoes to the outfielders, and coach third base. In addition I was given a uniform and an actual spot on the roster. Occasionally, only eight guys would show for a game and I was pressed into service. No one expected anything of me as a player, so there was no pressure or derision when I lived up to my abilities.

One weekend we played the nearby Carmichael team. As I was preparing balls and bats for the game, I looked across the diamond when our opponents began arriving on our field. Can you guess who the coach of the Carmichael squad was? Why, it was none other than Ron Tucker, star of stage, screen, and my worst nightmares. Each time I approached the plate to retrieve a team-mate's bat, I wondered if he would remember me. He gave no hint of recognition. Just as well, I figured.

Later in the game, one of our players had to leave early and I was pressed into service. I took the vacant outfield spot, butchered a routine fly, then trudged in for what would be my only time at bat. As I approached the plate in my loose-fitting uniform, the youngest and smallest player on the field, a boy among men, one who truly did not belong, I looked over at Coach Tucker. He stared away, betraying nothing, then spat a long stream of rich, brown toxic waste onto the ground. Hundreds of worms around the vis-itor's dugout gave their lives that day.

As I took my practice cuts, trying my best to look like I belonged, Tucker stepped out of the dugout and shouted to his pitcher for all the world to hear, "Three straight ones, Jimmy!" This was followed by a gliding hand motion to signify, "Just put it past him. He can't hit." Had I been in his position, I would have given my pitcher the same advice. But I would have called time-out and delivered the message privately so as not to humiliate the batter.

I was seething and refused to acknowledge the man. There was nothing more that I wanted in the world than to pound a long double into the gap and stand on second, glaring at my former coach. Nothing more except, perhaps, to swing so late that a foul shot would ricochet off his kneecap and hit him in the mouth, knocking a tooth or two loose. When Paramount films my life story, that's the way this at-bat will be portrayed. My teammates will lift me on their shoulders, and his players will be rolling, along with Tucker, on the dugout floor with tears of laughter streaming down their dusty Carmichael cheeks.

But life is not a movie. Jimmy threw three straight hard ones past my desperate bat. The manager of McClellan's American Legion team returned to the bench and sat down, as Paul Simon had so eloquently characterized another beaten athlete, "in his anger and his shame."

Nearly thirty years have passed since I played hardball for the last time. There were many good and special moments I retain from the game that are now inextricably woven into the fabric of my life. But there are a few I have not been able to shake, their shadows hanging long and cold like darkened clouds overhead, occasionally blocking out joy, muting the thunder of a short, unremarkable playing career.

A voice comes down from the cloud, its soothing tones coaxing me into uneasy fellowship. *You have a* right, it purrs. *Something precious was stolen and you have a* right *to be angry*.

I know this voice. It is as seductive as it is persuasive. It slinks into my heart like a wisp of perfume trailing a rare and beautiful woman. It is as cool and calculated as the odds on a Vegas jackpot. There is usually a kernel of selective truth nestled somewhere in its argument. This is the insidious nature of the beast—accurate information wrapped around a lie—a kind of candy-coated arsenic for the soul. The peril lies in the temptation to follow the voice's often reasonable-sounding suggestions.

This is the same voice, playing both sides of the fence, that told me I was no good, had no talent, had become worthless as a player. Once I began listening to this heartless voice, my playing skills began eroding measurably. I have often wondered how much better I might have become if I hadn't listened, if I hadn't believed the compelling testimony of this Deceiver. Certainly I lacked the tools to play professionally. But high school varsity ball was not entirely out of the question.

◆

My wife, Sally, is a gifted singer and communicator of the gospel. Several times a year she is invited to minister at a place in Wickenburg, Arizona, called Remuda Ranch. Remuda is a facility devoted to the treatment of anorexia and bulimia that boasts Christ-centered therapy as the means for overcoming these vicious syndromes.

In this place there are women who, by any standard, would be considered attractive, even beautiful, who have come to believe that they are ugly. There are ninety-pound adult patients convinced they are fat. For many, skipping a meal is a means to physical redemption. It is not uncom-

I know this voice. It is as seductive as it is persuasive. It slinks into my heart like a wisp of perfume trailing a rare and beautiful woman.

mon for women, prior to entering the treatment center, to take dozens of laxatives a day, keeping the calories off in search of the perfect self-image. Needless to say, this practice is devastating to their vital organs.

Sally shares with these ladies the story of her own wounded past—how she was bitten on the face by a dog at eight years old; how she heard the taunts of classmates who, one hundred stitches later, referred to her as "Scarface"; how she listened to these lies and, through some twisted form of reasoning, allowed them into her heart and began to own them.

Usually this story grabs the attention of the women and allows Sally to speak more directly into their lives. "Your bodies," she tells them, "have become testimony to the power of a lie."

Of course, she is right. The Great Deceiver would take the truth and distort it for his own evil ends. He doesn't fight fair. He will take his victory any way he can get it. His is a voice that compels a vital, healthy woman to starve her body in the futile quest to become the living embodiment of Barbie.

Less dramatically, he leads one person to do nothing more than discourage another. Simple. No big deal. But the lingering disappointment festers. Confidence is replaced by self-doubt. Gifting atrophies. Before long, a single unkind act or word strewn into one man's orchard yields a hard and bitter fruit. Another man comes along and samples the bad fruit, and the pattern of negativity continues.

So how do we break the cycle? Do we plug our ears and place blinders over our eyes? Such an attempt would be foolish, for the Enemy, given permission, has the power to speak into our hearts and sear images into our brains.

When we look into the mirror and, in the reflection, see a distortion of the truth, do we then keep looking into that glass darkly? If we do, we run the risk of falling in love—or at least becoming exceedingly comfortable—with the broken image.

With almost every situation I stumble across in my daily grind, I encounter a moment of choice. How I react in that instant to the circumstance determines the direction of the resolution.

I stub my toe on a rock. It really hurts. I can swear a blue streak. I can yell at a dog. I can kick a garbage can.[*]

The bottom line is, I own the moment of choice.

I can give the moment over to Satan, or I can choose to redeem it by offering it up to God. We have seen the former in the illustration above. As for the latter, I am not suggesting some wimpy, pseudo-Christian solution, the likes of which we see far too often in media depicting Christian life:

"I thank Thee, God, for rocks and stones. And for placing this particular rock in my path today, I give Thee thanks for a remarkable encounter with this breaker of mine toe."

No, I mean something much more real and substantive:

"Father, You know my toe is hurting big time right now. And I want to yell, not in pain, but in anger. Who *put* this crummy rock here, anyway? Oh yeah—You did. Please ease the throbbing, Lord, and help me to resist the temptation of giving in to my baser instincts. Take the anger from my heart, God, and replace it with your peace."

When we look into the mirror and, in the reflection, see a distortion of the truth, do we then keep looking into that glass darkly? If we do, we run the risk of falling in love—or at least becoming exceedingly comfortable—with the broken image.

The choice is simple. Listen to the voice whose sweet talk led to the fall of humankind in the Garden of Eden, or follow the heart of the One who promised, "I will never leave you or forsake you."

God is always there for us. He takes no vacations, shuts down

---

[*] I really don't recommend this as healing therapy for a stubbed toe. But then, every season, invariably, five or six major-league pitchers angrily leave games in which they have pitched poorly, punch out a concrete wall, and end up on the disabled list. I believe this reveals something profound about the disturbing trend of violence toward inanimate objects. I just have no idea what that revelation is.

no office for the weekend. Like an all-night answering service, He is open 24/7.

He was there on a baseball field as I was being spoon-fed lies about my relative worth. He was there in the quiet of my room as I pondered the downward spiral of my physical talents. He was there when I chose to believe the lie, and He permitted me that option.

My daughter Dusty listened to the story of my two coaches. She appreciated Mr. Barclay and thought Mr. Tucker heartless. She started to get angry in my defense and wanted to know: If my former Babe Ruth coach were still alive, what would I say to him today?

Usually such questions require time and thought, especially when you are trying to model truth as an important value to a twelve-year-old. But I knew the answer almost before the question left her lips.

Privately, I had already made my peace with Mr. Tucker. I won't really portray him writhing in agony during my upcoming bio-pic. Whatever frost of anger had once fallen on my heart has long since melted and is flowing into a stream of forgiveness. God is the source of this healing. I take no credit. His is an ocean of love and forgiveness. Mine is just a little creek, encrusted with moss and overflowing with polliwogs. But I am working on it.

To Mr. Barclay*, I would say thank you. Thanks for believing in me before I had the vision to do that for myself. I learned a good deal of my work ethic from you. And you always had a smile for me.

To Mr. Tucker—I would have liked to have been more a part of your team. Youth league coaches don't get paid, and I think you must have cared an awful lot about baseball to volunteer as much time to the game as you did. I just wish you had cared more about kids and less about winning. But who knows, in another time and place, you may have been the loner on the end of the bench,

---

* A photograph of Mr. Barclay appears in the upper right corner of page 72.

believing the lies told by a maimer of young hearts and a destroyer of dreams.

It has been said that time heals all wounds. While this is an oversimplification, time does afford us the opportunity to receive healing from the One who knows better than anyone about mending wounds and healing broken hearts.

As for me, having come around the far side of the mountain and still adjusting to living outside its shadow of a lie, I am learning to live my life not for the praise of men but for the glory of God.

The opposition is still out there, whether in the form of a disembodied voice or the incessant chatter of the infield as I step up to take my turn at bat. From here on, I just want to keep my eyes open, my reflexes sharp, and take the best darn cuts I can at that curve ball they keep trying to slip by me.

I'm due, baby. There's a ball out there with my name on it, and I need to believe that if I keep swinging, someday she'll find the sweet spot on my bat. Then high and deep is her address. You've gotta have a dream, right? Because…you know what?

Youneverknow.

A word aptly spoken
is like apples of gold
in settings of silver.
—*Proverbs 25:11*

To a ballplayer the game is a seed he planted as a child, a kind of beautiful creeping ivy that he was delighted to have entwine him. As an adult, he felt supported in every sense— financial, emotional, psychic—by his green, rich, growing game, just as ivy can strengthen a brick wall. But ivy, given time, can overpower and tear down a house.

—Thomas Boswell

Sixth Inning

Solo

During the early to mid-sixties, while navigating the perilous path to posterity, I tripped and fell into the gaping pothole of self-sufficiency. Somewhere between Roger Maris's sixty-first home run and the day Juan Marichal took a bat to Johnny Roseboro's head, I began realizing I didn't really need anyone other than me to have a good time playing the games I once enjoyed sharing with others. It seemed a harmless enough conceit. But if submerging myself in me was the ticket to a world where games could be experienced on an intense new level, it was also a whirlpool that would pull me down into its vortex. That I was able to come back up for air before I suffocated is more a measure of God's grace and mercy than my own wisdom or discernment.

I grew up a Kennedy Democrat. I bought into the Camelot myth while the paint on the castle was fresh and the scaffolding still in place. After the assassination, I mourned with Caroline and John-John before voting for LBJ in our fourth-grade mock election. What was I going to do—vote for some old guy from Arizona whose initials didn't even *rhyme* with JFK? When you are ten years old, political analysis only goes so far. Then it's time for the cartoons.

Ours was a clan of both registered and undocumented Democrats. We were loyal to our party, even when we had no idea what it stood for. With Watergate and Haight-Ashbury still off in the sociopolitical distance, I was a loyal foot soldier on the O'Connor way of life. I voted O'Connor, I worshiped O'Connor, I thought O'Connor. Even as the Beatles were premiering their mop-tops on American sod, I figured Nat King Cole and Jerry Vale were the coolest cats around. That's right—I even *listened* O'Connor. So it was ironic that my slide down the slippery slope of family rebellion started not with the bad-boy music of the sassy, strutting Mick or the cradle-robbing Jerry Lee, but with listening to that all-American band leader of the club that's made for you and me—Walt Disney.

Either for Christmas or for my birthday, I was given a copy of a children's album, *Walt Disney's Fun with Music*. It was filled with all manner of riotous, rollicking good times and romping, delicious delights made semi-famous on the afternoon kids' show *The Mickey Mouse Club*.

Sing-alongs. Parade marches. Cubby O'Brien pounding out his best Buddy Rich licks on bass drum. More sing-alongs. More marches. Jimmy Dodd pitching the virtues of Mouseketeering. Anthems. Fireworks. Bobby Burgess tap-dancing—on a record, no less! At full throttle, he sounded exactly like…Cubby O'Brien pounding out his best Buddy Rich licks on bass drum.

Fun with Music was 33-1/3 revolutions per minute of musical nitro. Blasting our senses through large, felt-covered, black-eared frivolity, this Disney album was simply too much of a hot-time hoot for a kid to safely assimilate in one afternoon.

Uptempo, uplifting, upbeat. This uproarious musical extravaganza could easily have been dubbed *Up with Short People!* For it packed in its musical syringe a potent dose of the controlled substance that Mickey Mouse had begun hawking in every home, in every store, on every corner of Main Street, U.S.A.: happiness! Ear-to-ear smiles frozen in Grauman's cement. Audio saccharine with a sugar chaser.

There was one exception. One song—a ballad—bolted from the pack and demanded that attention be paid because it was so entirely different from every other track on the album. A redwood in the Christmas tree lot. Lawrence Olivier in a high school production of *Guys and Dolls*.

The singer was an astonishing talent. A diva by any measure, so long as teenage boys were holding the yardstick. Her name was Annette Funicello, but to her legion of faithful fans, we prepubescent moths drawn inexorably to her eternal, searing flame each weekday afternoon at 3:30, she had no last name. She was simply Annette. Any attempt to identify her beyond those two syllables would have been as silly as asking the record store clerk for the latest release by Liberace Jones.

The song was called "I'm All Alone at Coney Island." Annette delivered the tune with heart and conviction. In industry terms, she "sold it." She sang about being at Coney Island. Alone. Hundreds of people on the boardwalk, but not a single boy to come along and take hold of her hand.

How awful. An American tragedy.

A cynic could look at Annette's dateless Coney Island dilemma and brand it a master stroke of hormonal manipulation by Uncle Walt. I mean, this teenage Cleopatra, this New Frontier version of Britney Spears, is riding the merry-go-round at a densely populated amusement park and can't seem to find a suitable companion to buy her a corn dog.

Sure. Uh-huh. Right.

All I know is that I could not have been the only boy who heard the winsome Annette singing, "I'm All Alone…" and suddenly began rifling through his piggy bank, plotting fantasy travel itineraries involving TWA, Greyhound, and Yellow Cab. There must have been thousands of us.

But I never gave a thought to the others. For I was certain Annette was singing only to me.

Like Annette, I understood all too well the mechanics of solitude. You can be rowing a boat solo in the middle of Lake Tahoe on a moonlit summer's night and still feel the presence and warmth of those closest to you. You can also be standing in Times Square at midnight on New Year's Eve and be totally alone. That was how I perceived myself between kindergarten and junior high. An odd duck. Alone in a rowboat in the middle of Times Square.

Any attempt to identify her beyond those two syllables would have been as silly as asking the record store clerk for the latest release by Liberace Jones.

I grew up in an atmosphere that was not terribly conducive to outside friendships. My parents, though they loved me and provided for my physical needs, had very little idea how to get along with each other. Some would call it arguing. I always thought of their friction as Olympic-level interpersonal debate. Their filibusters, generally loud and long, spilled over into the lives of my sisters and me, making home an uncomfortable environment to share with classmates. I made a few friends in school and Little League. I spent time at their houses, but without home-field reciprocation most of these relationships eventually unraveled like a bald tire hitting a nail at 70 miles per hour.

Sure, I had sisters, but they were perennially four and nine years younger than me. And besides, they were, uh…well, *girls*. We tried playing games together. I taught them Monopoly, Parcheesi, chess, and various card games. Because of the age difference I almost always won and, eventually, grew bored with them.

So I turned inward. Somewhere along the way I realized that I could be my own best companion. I began to play my own special brand of games. Games against myself. Contests where I participated simultaneously as champion and challenger, whose resolutions painted me equally as victor and vanquished.

For a while it was a process of trial and error. Solitaire Monopoly was difficult to pull off, as it usually involved trading. Trading involved judgment. And judgment allowed for a certain amount of discretion in the area of fairness. It was far too easy to trade away Baltic Avenue and receive Boardwalk when my only accountability was to myself.

For games of solitaire to really work well, they have to be contests with few optional areas—more black and white than gray. So it was natural I would turn my attention to baseball, the fairest game I knew.

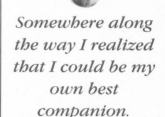

Somewhere along the way I realized that I could be my own best companion.

Between the ages of nine and fourteen, when I wasn't out actually *playing* the game with kids my age, I invented baseball contests with a tennis or Wiffle ball, whichever was handy.

The games weren't terribly complicated. I threw or hit a ball up on the roof of our house from about twenty feet back. Then I would run under the eaves, keeping a steady eye on the shingles, an alert ear for the ball rolling down the wooden slope. Because there was no way to see the ball at that point, I had to rely on my hearing to follow its course.

As the ball hit the roof, I scampered in and listened for it picking up momentum on the long brown slanted track. A three-car choo-choo at first—*clickety-clack*, *clickety-clack*—then gradually building steam like a freight locomotive until it roared past the final shingle and began its perilous descent to the bridgeless chasm below.

If I had judged distance, sound, and aerodynamics correctly, I would be set in place for the easiest of catches. Sometimes, though, an unseen nail or rogue shingle would change the ball's trajectory and a new path was dictated. Because I wasn't privy to the shift, I would often, at the final second, be forced to leap parallel to the ground in a heroic attempt to pull the ball back into my outstretched body before hitting the ground full force, my elbows and knees eventual martyrs to the cause.

It was a glorious game, this Roofball. I invented players and teams, borrowing liberally from the ones that already existed in the major leagues. I played out several teams' entire schedules. Then, before you knew it, the World Series would come along to punctuate another splendid season.

I also discovered many other solo amusements to fill my endless summer hours. Dice and spinner games were all the rage in the sixties, and I found three that fit my taste and needs.

◆

All-Star Baseball—This was an early attempt at a realistic simulation game. An actual major-league player's statistics were boiled down to general probabilities based on the previous season's at-bats. A player's card consisted of a light cardboard circle, maybe 3.5 inches in diameter. The center portion was cut out so the card could be placed over the spinner and fit snugly against a hard cardboard base. Once set, I, the manager, would flick the spinner and watch it orbit the card. A good, strong spin bode well for the batter. A weak and wobbly one was cause for concern and sometimes would be stopped intentionally before the play was official so that a good, hearty re-spin could be allowed. If a batter had a history of hitting lots of home runs, the corresponding area on his card would be wider than that of a weak-hitting shortstop. If he was known to strike out a lot, his range for missing pitches would also be reflected. The weakness of this game, while it was fairly literal in its portrayal of offense, was that there was no accommodation for pitching. A hurler was in the lineup in name only—his strikeouts, walks, and earned run average were never taken into account.

I invented players and teams, borrowing liberally from the ones that already existed in the major leagues. I played out several teams' entire schedules.

Strat-O-Matic Baseball—This game used dice instead of spinners. Strat-O-Matic was a mail-order phenomenon that was much more precise than All-Star Baseball in its replication of a player's previous statistical season. Serious research was put into these cards by the manufacturer's crack team of statisticians with their actuarial tables and probability formulas. In theory, an entire major league season could be played following the exact schedule of the real teams, and the results would be astoundingly similar. Pitchers' stats were as important as hitters' numbers, so a team that threw future Hall-of-Famer Tom Seaver against journeyman pitcher Bob Bolin would have a decided advantage in the game's outcome—just as in real life. In addition, player injury, ballpark, and weather factors also came into play. Strat-O-Matic was a complicated and time-consuming game to play, but the esthetic rewards and thrilling realism made this the Rolls Royce of baseball board games.

Peg Baseball—If Strat-O-Matic was a luxury vehicle, Peg Baseball was the Volkswagen of simulated baseball. Also a dice game, Peg Baseball's playing board consisted of a baseball diamond drawn on a cardboard platform fitting snugly in the game box. There was a hole large enough for a small wooden peg at first, second, and third base. These pegs, when placed in their appropriate holes, represented runners on the basepaths. A batter with a perplexing smile and generic uniform was drawn permanently standing at home plate. Unlike the other two, Peg Baseball did not rely on or attempt to replicate a major-league player's true numbers. The game was simplicity itself. There were two dice with possible combinations of two through twelve. Roll a 2-3 or 2-5 and you had yourself a single. 2-2 was a double and 3-3 a triple. 1-6 represented an error, 4-5 a base on balls, and 6-6, presumably the hardest combination to roll, cleared the bases with a home run. Everything else was an out of one kind or another. The beauty of the game was once you learned Peg Baseball's short list of variables, you no longer needed the board if you could remember the score and calculate the on-base situation in your head. To this day, whenever I see a couple of dice, I don't look for a Monopoly game, and I don't get the urge to pack up the car and head for the green felt tables of Nevada. I see scoreboards, I envision box scores, my pulse quickens, and I think, "Come on, double sixes!"

◆

The games themselves were only half the fun and excitement. They were, after all, only mass-produced, prefab cardboard houses built on foundations of chance or skill. What set many box baseball games apart from the likes of Uno or Yahtzee was the level to which a player chose to be involved. As kids we *played* Stratego and Risk, but we *lived* for Strat-O-Matic. How deep were you willing to go for the sake of the game?

A Scrabble aficionado might play ten games a day. But does she fancy herself as Professor Madeline Heath, world famous lexicographer and linguist? Of course not. She plays the game as herself and takes great personal pride in her triple word scores and seven-letter combinations.

But in All-Star Baseball, I *became* the manager who determined the lineups and facilitated substitutions. Playing Strat-O-Matic, I *was* the general manager who worked on improving the club by making trades with other teams. At times I even picked out a generic player card, writing the name Mike O'Connor on it and inserting myself into an all-star line-up that included Ken Boyer, Ernie Banks, and Roberto Clemente. I was activated purely for the good of the club, you understand.

As kids we played Stratego and Risk, but we lived for Strat-O-Matic. How deep were you willing to go for the sake of the game?

There were other duties to perform in the running of a sports franchise. Somebody needed to be the official scorer and team statistician. Let Mikey do it. Batting averages, home runs, and runs batted in were scrupulously maintained in a small pocket spiral notebook and audited annually by Price Waterhouse. Pitching records in the green spiral, hitting archives in the red. Hey, I would have been out in the stands hawking hot dogs if the Board of Health hadn't shut down our concession operations.

When I was eleven, my parents gave me what, at the time, seemed like the greatest gift of my life. No larger than a Swanson's TV dinner tray, my new Radio Shack reel-to-reel tape recorder was a portal to another dimension of baseball fulfillment. I had, of course, been "broadcasting" games into a balled-up sock attached to a ruler for a couple of years before receiving this technological marvel. Now there would not only be a permanent record of the events in the KBAT Radio vault, but my mother would no longer need to enlist bounty hunters to round up my fugitive footwear.

With the addition of this new equipment, we were able to go into the dugout and onto the field for our Manor Drugstore Pre- and Postgame Interview. ("Next time you're in the Foothill Farms area, be sure to drop in and say hi to the friendly folks at Manor Drug.") Being shorthanded in the broadcast booth, I was obliged not only to ask but also answer each question. After deepening my high-pitched voice as the interviewer, I then offered my best southern drawl as the Georgia-native third baseman who belted tonight's prodigious upper deck blast—all the while blushing at the mention of his ninth inning heroics. ("Shucks, Maaahk, Ah wuz jess glad tuh hev a small paht 'n this 'ere tracter pull. Nuthin' sweeter 'n a win, ceptin' mama's sweet tater pah. Heh-heh! They's twenty-fav gahs on this 'ere team and we cain't git to the Serious withinout each and ever one of 'em 'tributin' each in they own way 'cordin' to the gifs the Good Lawd give 'em. Ah'm jess one gah, Maaahk.")

"Excellence in broadcasting" may be a modern-day slogan, but it was a code to which I had committed decades before Rush Limbaugh.

◆

During my college days, I read a book written by Robert Coover entitled *The Universal Baseball Association: J. Henry Waugh, Prop*. In his novel, Coover revealed a man, Henry Waugh, who had created an entire baseball league—much as I had done many times as a child. There was one significant difference. This was a full-grown man. A man who had a job. A man who often stayed home from work to play the day's league schedule on his kitchen table. A man whose sole reason for showing up at work, it seemed, was to pay the rent and electricity bills, without which there would be no stadium for his teams to play in and no lights for the night games.

Henry used fictional names for his players, never once dipping his toe into the major-league talent pool as I had. They were given colorful monikers—Damon Rutherford, Skeeter Parson, Chauncey O'Shea—names that seemed to have escaped from a 1930s detective novel. Names that simply *reeked* of character.

During the first season of the Universal Baseball Association, it struck Henry as odd that these ballplayers with the great names had no personal histories to speak of. They had, after all, just been created. As the season progressed, he began writing the life story of each player: hometown, number of children, wife's name, favorite foods. Was he a snappy dresser? A klutz off the field? Did he visit sick kids in the hospital on his days off? These were the questions Henry felt the fans of the UBA wanted to know, so he obligingly filled in the blanks.

As the seasons progressed and entire careers played out on Henry's tabletop, it became apparent that his players would, eventually, need to retire, making way for incoming crops of rookies. Truth be told, if the game were to accurately mirror life, a few players from the heralded UBA past would need to die. Setting up a life-insurance actuarial table as a guideline, Henry started new seasons with special rolls of the dice to determine who would retire and who, among the old-timers, would pass on to their final reward. As a fitting tribute, Henry wrote a detailed obituary for each, peppering the article with little-known stories from the player's career, his off-field interests including civic organizations he belonged to, the cause of death, and, of course, his next of kin.

"Excellence in broadcasting" may be a modern-day slogan, but it was a code to which I had committed decades before Rush Limbaugh.

It was this last bit—the writing of each player's obituary—that equally compelled me to get lost in Henry's world and to be utterly repulsed by it. The hairs stood up on the back of my neck while reading the detail through which he allowed himself to be pulled into each player's life. The obsession was scary even to one who was, himself, obsessed with baseball.

Henry was losing himself in the process. You could almost see him disappearing down his kitchen sink, dice roll by dice roll, until his march to oblivion was just a Drano treatment away. This man had lost himself so completely in his game that he often had difficulty distinguishing fantasy from reality. I had been down this path as a boy. I had rolled the dice. I had broadcast the games. I had even fleshed out some of the details of batters' lives. But the players never died on my watch. And I never wrote their obituaries.

But even as his life was circling the drain, Henry realized something was missing, that his life was somehow incomplete. So he invited someone in—a part-time girlfriend to join him in the game, to help make his hours more fulfilling and less lonely. She thought it strange for a grown man to be involved with such a solitary activity, yet she was willing to give it a shot if it meant spending more time with and drawing closer to Henry.

But she didn't understand baseball. She had no concept of the hit-and-run, the suicide squeeze, or the infield fly rule, and she had little patience for Henry explaining the intricacies of them to her. She was content to roll the dice and cheer. Henry could not hide his disdain. Why would you be satisfied to paint by numbers when you had Picasso as a mentor? Clearly, she would not be his long-term companion in this pursuit.

❖

The fictional Henry Waugh and I were not alone in our obsession. Literally thousands upon thousands of young boys have used baseball, in one form or another, to pull away from the world—blocking out what may be a deep and private pain they probably have not fully understood. I have read their books. I have talked to them as men. One thing is clear. We thought we were alone. We thought no one else in the universe would do something as insane as broadcasting a baseball game into a balled-up sock on a ruler. As it turns out, we were a nation of disconnected computers searching for our network. We were unwitting participants in the world's largest solitaire tournament.

What is it that seduced us to lose ourselves willingly, whole-heartedly in this quest for phantom hits, runs, and errors? Why were we driven inward, embracing baseball for one when baseball for two or six or twelve or eighteen not only works better but is prefer-able and infinitely more fulfilling?

Isn't it obvious? We were trying to replace something that was missing. We were attempting to replenish the supply of a commodity we could hardly define yet instinctively under-stood had been left out of the equa-tion.

Blaise Pascal, the noted seven-teenth-century French mathematician and philosopher, once wrote, "There is a God-shaped vacuum in every heart." I know this is true. I know it because, like others my age, I have tried to pack that hole in my heart with all manner of filler over the years.

Literally thou-sands upon thou-sands of young boys have used baseball, in one form or another, to pull away from the world.... I have talked to them as men. One thing is clear. We thought we were alone.

First we tried the candy store: "Gimme some M&Ms, some Juicy Fruit, a PayDay, a Mounds, two Almond Joys, five Reeses, three Snickers, a-a-a-nd twenty-seven pounds of Jujubes."

Then we moved on to the toy store, because you know we boys just love our toys. We caught Frisbee fever and we picked up Stix. We sizzled for Hot Wheels and we bent over backward for Twister. We flipped for pinball and we fought over G.I. Joe.

When that didn't fill us, we moved on to more grown-up pur-suits: work, love, relationships—some tried drugs, others alco-hol. We filled and we filled and we filled, but the holes in our hearts were still as empty as that first day in the candy store.

And why not?

We had tried just about everything. Everything, that is, except the one and only commodity that could have filled our heart's vacuum. Yes, some of us had even tasted of God's goodness—or at least thought we had—before turning our backs on our Creator for things of this world that seemed more attractive and felt more substantial. However, as we knocked on their doors of admittance, these idols proved hollow and empty, their echoes rippling in the wind until the next great thing came along to grab our hearts and attention.

When Henry Waugh realized his game—indeed, his life—was lacking for having no one to share it with, he called upon his girlfriend to partake in his tabletop dream. He was looking for someone who could fill up the empty place in his heart. But she was ill-equipped for any role in Henry's salvation.

◆

Like Annette, I was all alone, looking for someone to come along and take hold of my hand. One day someone did. She not only walked with me arm in arm, but she helped me to see the emptiness of my life as I had lived it. She showed me the fullness God had for me, far beyond games I had played or the fantasy worlds I might create.

A few years back, while cleaning out a closet, I discovered my old game of All-Star Baseball. The box was dusty and wrinkled. I lifted the top and flicked the spinner once or twice. The old girl still worked. I thought about pulling out some disks and playing a few games. Only for a moment. Then I replaced the lid on the box and set it in the pile for the Salvation Army pickup. Like an old friend you meet at a twenty-five-year reunion, I just needed to say hello before I realized we had very little left in common.

I no longer prefer to play games by myself. More than ever I am enjoying the company of others. This is, after all, the way God designed us. Fellowship is a need of the human heart, a component of the God-shaped vacuum.

I heard Annette finally found someone and settled down. Good for her. I couldn't expect her to pine over me forever. I only hope she has forgiven me for not coming to her rescue with a bouquet of cotton candy all those years ago. Turns out my piggy bank was hoarding nickels and pennies. Hardly enough to rescue a damsel in distress three thousand miles away.

I'm doing OK myself. Life is full and rich. There's a song in my heart…a hand holding mine…and I'm not alone at Coney Island.

The Lord God said,
"It is not good for man to be alone."
—Genesis 2:18

*Everyone is aware of the Calvinist nature,
the sense of foreboding that attaches itself
to the Red Sox.*

—*Roger Angell*

Seventh-Inning Stretch

Selections from Sally Klein's Prayer Journal

With two outs and the count two balls and one strike, the young pitcher, Calvin Schiraldi, stared past New York Mets catcher Gary Carter into the waiting glove of his own catcher, Rich Gedman. The team had come too far to be denied now—178 games plus 68 years, to be exact. Since 1918, the last year they had won it all, the Boston Red Sox had become experts at the art of snatching defeat from the jaws of victory. And here they were again. Tenth inning, Game Six. The 1986 World Series. Nervously studying the jagged teeth in their opponent's gaping mouth. Wasn't it Preacher Roe who defined this moment? "Sometimes you eat the bear," he waxed. "Sometimes the bear eats you."

It's not as if this franchise was built on a foundation of failure. The Sox had a proud and storied tradition of winning. In the nearly seven decades since their last world championship, they had appeared in their share of World Series games. No, these were not Chicago's Cubs. But neither were they New York's Yankees.

Boston had become your old Uncle Mort—a career salesman with a fabled history of commissions, a wall full of awards, and a hundred stories attached to each. But Mort was getting up there now. His arthritic hip kept him from calling on as many leads as he had in his glory days. His mind, once a steel trap that mercilessly closed on a prospect until the sale was extracted, now had difficulty holding a thought. His colleagues at the office were cruel. They told Mort-stories behind his back until the laughter hurt and somebody hollered, "Stop, yer killin' me!" Everyone knew the sad truth about Mort. He could pull in a commission here and there. He could cold-call and track a lead without embarrassing himself too badly. But he could no longer eat the bear.

Such was the tenuous spot in which the 1986 Boston club found itself. While fifty thousand hometown New Yorkers made obligatory noise, they pretty much knew their Mets were finished. The specter of defeat sat off on the horizon, pulling on socks and cleats for his customary post-game trot around the bases. But the Sox were chasing ghosts of their own.

In 1920, Boston owner Harry Frazee sold star player Babe Ruth outright to the Yankees for the princely sum of $100,000. Since closing that deal, the Yanks had gone on to become a dynasty the likes of which no other baseball team has ever surpassed. The Red Sox, on the other hand, had gone on to win numerous American League pennants but had never again held the coveted World Series trophy. This anomaly has since become known in baseball circles as "The Curse of the Bambino."

In the lingo of commerce, the Boston Red Sox could no longer close the big sale. Calvin Schiraldi knew all this, of course, as he looked in for his catcher's sign. He understood that 68-plus years of misfortune—whether at the hands of Ruth, bad luck, or even fate—were about to dissipate into the New York skyline if only he could induce Carter to hit the ball *at* someone. Or, better yet, to strike out. With two outs, no runners, and the Mets down by two in extra innings, Schiraldi knew the odds were in his favor. Maybe even a million to one.

I sat at home in my Glendale, California, apartment, drinking in this sparkling moment of baseball history. For once in my life, I was a dispassionate observer. Normally, I would be rooting for the National League team all the way—such was my loathing for the designated-hitter rule employed by the American League. But this year I had a girlfriend—my on-again-off-again fiancée, Sally—who was such a huge Sox fan that I could not find it in my heart—or my best interests—to root against her. So I sat on the fence and watched with fascination as history unfolded.

Little did I realize, as I watched Schiraldi's careful windup, that it was not only baseball's memoir that was being written in this critical moment but, indeed, a new chapter of my own. Had I understood that my involvement in this game was anything more than having two eyes glued to the tube, I might have gone running into the night, babbling incoherently. Instead, I inserted a potato chip into the appropriate orifice and waited.

What happened next…changed the course of my life forever.

◆

I left Sacramento in 1982 to pursue fame and fortune. If I couldn't have both, finding either would have been acceptable. For two years I had been shooting demos of my songs out into the deepest parts of the galaxy—Nashville and Los Angeles—black holes of the entertainment industry to a musical neophyte like me. But all I ever got back in the mail were rejection letters—*form* rejection letters. It finally occurred to me that if I ever wanted to receive constructive criticism from bona fide professionals in my chosen field—if I wanted to casually bump into Barbra Streisand over lunch or wrestle Kenny Rogers' producer to the ground, pinning him hopelessly to the floor with one arm while I slipped my cassette demo into his sound system with the other—then I needed to be living in outer space.

In May I jettisoned the Sacramento comforts of home and friends to begin floating in the weightless environment that was L.A. Finally, I would be able to interact in a meaningful way with the song-writing community. The question was, would they be willing to interact in a meaningful way with me?

On the journey south I brought with me varying amounts of youth, talent, enthusiasm, and my father's cash. Helping to focus these disparate gifts into a cohesive force was the secret weapon I had dared whisper to no one—my guaranteed no-questions-asked, double-your-money-back, one-year success plan. At the end of my first twelve months, I was going to own this town.

Little did I realize, as I watched Schiraldi's careful windup, that it was not only baseball's memoir that was being written in this critical moment but, indeed, a new chapter of my own.

Forgetting for the moment that guys named Spielberg and Lucas already owned this town and were unlikely to yield it without a court order signed by God, my short-term goal was to have at least one hit record sung by a well-known recording artist by the end of the first year in my exciting new Hollywood existence. Despite the fact that I am currently in the nineteenth year of my one-year plan and that guys named Spielberg, Katzenberg, Geffen, and Lucas now own this town, I haven't given up. I believe that even if I never lunch with Barbra, Providence could smile upon me, and I may yet accidentally dent the fender of husband James Brolin's car. If, while exchanging license and insurance information, a song demo should mysteri-ously find its way into his tape player—what would be the harm?

Hey, have you ever *heard* James Brolin sing?

Looking for a core group of fellow writers and advanced training in the art of putting music and words together, I enrolled in an adult extension course at Cal State-Northridge in the San Fernando Valley. Each week our teacher, Jack Segal, whose songwriting credits included "Scarlet Ribbons" and "When Sunny Gets Blue," allowed us to bring one tune from our drawer of old songs and offer it up on the altar of public criticism. In a class of roughly twenty-five budding writers, generally fifteen or so shared something with the class each week. It seemed I was a favorite of Jack's, so he heaped on the critical abuse with

> *Guys named Spielberg and Lucas already owned this town and were unlikely to yield it without a court order signed by God.*

an extra-large ladle, holding me to a high standard. I think he appreciated the fact that I was trying to write songs with meat and substance, something more than run-of-the-mill love songs.

There was another writer in the class who marched to the beat of her own drummer. From the first moment I heard Sally Klein sing, I knew there was an angel caught in her throat. She was writing a musical, *In Search of Prince Charming*. Each week Sally would debut a song she played live on the classroom piano. Each session I looked forward to the time she would unveil her newest piece. She wrote unique melodies and her lyrics were detailed paintings.

But her songs were not always pleasant. She wrote most of her melodies in a minor key. As I am a lyricist and not a musician, I could not lay my finger on the reason I felt uneasy at times during her songs. But I found many of her endings unsatisfactory— as if biting into a fine cut of prime rib that I was not allowed to swallow. While I loved her technique and craft, when I submitted my written comments, I noted that the themes she explored often seemed melancholy and without hope.

I, on the other hand, usually sent messages that were polar opposites of Sally's. "Thank You for the Ride" was a song that used Disneyland metaphors for a relationship facing its breakup. "Every Saturday Night" shared the plight of a woman who couldn't get a date to save her life. In each case, and in most of the songs I wrote, no matter how bleak the prospects of the protagonist in the first two verses, I would use the song's bridge to turn the corner and offer the listener some measure of redemption.

> *From the first moment I heard Sally Klein sing, I knew there was an angel caught in her throat.*

I remember receiving one of the critiques, which were always written in the margins of a lyric sheet we provided our classmates, offering the following comments: "You write beautifully. The craft is excellent. Clever ideas. But your continued insistence upon ending your songs on a hopeful note is unrealistic and misleading. Life is not like that." The comments were signed "S. K."

One evening, as class ended and I went about pulling my books and personal effects together, I realized someone was standing before my desk. Looking up, I was startled to find five-foot three-inch, brown-eyed brunette Sally Klein waiting patiently, wearing purple pants and matching suspenders.

"I like your writing" was all she said.

"Thank you," I replied. "I think you write amazing songs. I can't wait to hear the whole show."

"Thanks."

An awkward pause later she added, "Would you like to go out sometime for a cup of coffee?"

As a child, I had once tasted a sip of my mother's coffee. It not only held no appeal for me, I thought it was repulsive. A lifetime avoiding coffee-flavored foods ensued. And so, when Sally invited me out for coffee—to my taste the most reviled of all card-carrying members in the food chain—I naturally retorted, "Sure, that would be nice."

What can I say? She was cute and I probably would have joined her for a cup of battery acid.

After class one evening, Sally and I met at Tiny Naylor's Coffee Shop, which has since been torn down. So much for the sanctity of historical landmarks. We talked about songs. We talked about life. We commiserated over the verbal thrashings endured at the hands of our tough but well-meaning teacher. Before you could say, "Make those hash browns extra crispy," it was 6:00 A.M. Bleary-eyed, I paid the bill for dinner, breakfast, and hot chocolates till dawn. Turns out *she* didn't drink coffee either.

We began realizing, despite the fact that we had basic disagreements on a wide range of subjects, that there was one recurring theme through which we moved in step to the other's beat. We both loved songs. As serious writers who suffered the misfortune of plying their talent during the dance-music era, we believed lyrics were the soul of the song. Let others treat the words as innocent bystanders on the way to the Top 40—we had a message of truth and beauty to share. No one was going to force us to say, "Do-wah ditty dum-dum" in the chorus when the melody was screaming for richness and depth.

So we set about collaborating. Words and music: O'Connor & Klein. I liked the billing. In the process of writing several new songs, Sally and I became friends. Good and trusted friends. One ground rule we had laid out during our marathon cocoa-fest was that, even though we were both unattached, neither of us was looking for a relationship. So we signed on as co-writers who really liked each other. There would be none of that Burt Bacharach/Carole Bayer Sager I'm-in-love-with-my-collaborator nonsense for us. This is why, after watching the epic final episode of the beloved television series *M*A*S*H* together, having shared

Sally's only gourmet dish—tuna/mac casserole—we were both stunned when I, standing at her doorway, asked if I might kiss her good-night. Sally froze momentarily, while a wariness bordering on fear kidnapped her face. The exchange went something like:

"Kiss?"

"Yes."

"Now?"

"Yes."

"*Now*?"

"Yes."

"Where?"

"I thought the lips might be nice."

Tracy and Hepburn may have had snappier patter, but I would put our first peck up there with almost any pre-1960 screen kiss.

As winter turned to spring, my brain, which had been a finely tuned instrument of logic and rhyming, began turning to mush. I was in love—or at least deep like. I began spending all my free time with Sally, to the detriment of my one-year plan.

One of the first things I learned about her was that she was a tenacious seeker of truth. She tried to wrap her mind around many different philosophies in her formative and adult years. She started out her religious life attending an Orthodox synagogue with her family on the High Holy Days. When that proved too constrictive for her mother, Sally's family joined a Reformed synagogue. As she moved into her teens, Sally didn't see much point believing in a God who seemed so distant and disconnected from her life, so she stopped going altogether.

In college Sally opened her mind to Ayn Rand, a Russian-born writer who through her works formulated a philosophy called "objectivism." Rand celebrated the heroic in man, centering on the importance of self. Her views were the antithesis of Judeo-Christian values. Predictably, she was an atheist.

For a time Sally latched on to Ayn Rand and began to study

some of her teachings. It seemed to her, though, that Rand denounced the value of the underdog. Once a loser, always a loser. Was there no room for redemption? Sally felt that in Rand's eyes, *she* would be considered a loser too. She was soon disillusioned with a philosophy she saw as fraught with fallacy.

Sally's search for truth brought her to Zen. But, try as she might, Sally could never clear from her mind the eclectic clutter of thoughts that stood between her and the embrace of nothingness.

Somewhere along the line a friend named Ross gave Sally C. S. Lewis's classic *The Great Divorce*. Rich, a former boyfriend of Sally's, planted a copy of *Mere Christianity* on her bookshelf. Both of these guys were Jews who had accepted Jesus as their Messiah. One thing, however, Sally knew with certainty: Jesus was *not* the truth. Just about everyone in her life had told her so, from her rabbi to her parents. Still, here were these intelligent friends who had now anchored their existence to a man who had clearly lived—no one was denying that—yet claimed He was the Son of God, some two thousand years earlier.

As she read *The Great Divorce*, she recognized herself in one of Lewis's characters. In this allegorical tale there is a bishop who takes a bus ride to heaven. There he meets an old friend who invites him to come to meet God. Rather than jump at the invitation, the bishop argues and debates with his chum, attempting to justify his own standards and beliefs. In the end, he returns on the bus without ever meeting his Creator.

Sally possessed the argumentative qualities of the bishop—and she knew it. Feeling the conviction that often oozes from an anointed work, she decided to try to find God—to test Him on His home turf.

Because I had grown up in a church, Sally asked me to accompany her on this experiment of the Spirit. We picked a large congregation, figuring we could slip in and slip out unobtrusively. No such luck. One of the first things the pastor asked us to do was "turn to your neighbor and tell him 'God loves you.' " Although this sort of social engineering didn't sit well with us, at least we had the presence of mind to turn and address each other.

"God loves you," we said with the same kind of enthusiasm one exudes when facing a large plate of spinach. We rolled our eyes in unison.

"Now," continued the pastor, "turn to your *other* neighbor and tell *him* 'God loves you!' " Having just finished a whole plate of spinach, Sally and I were in no mood for collard greens. We turned outward and mumbled the appropriate phrase with no joy or conviction. We had done our duty—now could we *PLEASE SIT DOWN?!* Finally the puppeteer dropped the strings, and we flopped lifelessly into our chairs.

Now we remembered. It was this same type of pointless manipulation through peer pressure that had driven us, disillusioned, from the seats of organized religion years before. Where was the life in that church? Where was God?

Sally eventually waded through the deep waters of *Mere Christianity*. Finishing the book, she became angry. Lewis had said ethics and morals were not enough in life—that if you want to find truth you need to believe in the person of God through His Son, Jesus Christ, and no other way. Sally didn't even know if God existed. *But if He did,* she thought, *why would He give a rip about me? And why does* Jesus *have to be part of it?* Frustrated and then enraged, Sally challenged God—if, indeed, He existed—to make himself known to her. Having thrown the gauntlet down, she fell asleep.

The following day, January 2, 1984, Sally shared with me this account: "Last night I had a dream about a war. And you were in the dream. I needed to go fight the war, but you put down your shield and walked away. We were separated by the war and I was very sad.

"I woke up suddenly," she continued, "and the room was quiet. Then, for just a moment, I was filled with this overwhelming feeling of love. My heart, my head—every corner of my being was flooded by a love that had no shadow in it. I knew, beyond all my arguments, that this was God. His love was perfect and pure. He answered me."

Finally Sally had encountered the precious truth for which she had long searched. God had touched her in a real and personal way. She may have needed a little more convincing, but she wasn't likely to soon forget how God had enveloped her heart with the most tangible sense of love she had ever felt.

Caution was the road sign along her course of action. She started reading the Bible and attending church. Still, it was many weeks before she called God "Lord" in prayer. It took nine months before she finally used

> *It was this same type of pointless manipulation through peer pressure that had driven us, disillusioned, from the seats of organized religion years before.*

the "J" word. Being a Jew, Jesus was always the hardest name to say and the most difficult of all to acknowledge. The centuries of atrocities done to her people in His name seemed an impenetrable roadblock. Nevertheless, on October 6, 1984, in a small Messianic Jewish congregation in Beverly Hills, Sally asked Yeshua—Jesus—into her heart, into her life. Ironically, it was Yom Kippur, the Jewish Day of Atonement.

I had grown increasingly uncomfortable during Sally's quest. After spending the first fifteen years of my life in church, religion had left me cold. I equated God and religion equally; this was the breadth of my experience. You showed up at the appointed time, said a prayer, and ate a wafer. Hey, I could have done that in the school cafeteria. Was God in the bread? Everyone said He was. I didn't taste Him.

Sunday had no impact on the other six days in our lives. In fact, the sixty minutes we spent in church had no direct relation even to Sunday's other twenty-three hours. There was church—and there was everything else.

But where was God? I saw Him in the pictures on the wall. His name was up on the altar. The grown-ups had His name on their lips—at times it was even spoken reverently. We went to church because it was supposed to be good for us. Well, so was medicine, but we knew enough to take it more than once a week if we wanted to get better.

Mind you, I'm not saying God didn't show up on Sundays. I just don't think we knew where to look—or how to find Him. We were given prayers to memorize that we didn't really understand so we could recite together a request for something we didn't really want, petitioning Someone we didn't really know.

Even a young boy could see that our religion had gotten a little *too* organized and could use some serious chaos. What would happen if a pastor stopped his sermon in midparable and said, "Y'know…what I think I'm supposed to do right now is stop talking so we can all stand up … and wait to hear from God"? Would two hundred individual unrehearsed prayers from the heart cause so much dissonance that God might get a headache? Wouldn't it be a richer testimony if, instead of wearing our Sunday best, the knees in our corduroy trousers were smooth and almost worn through? What if our songs were prayers and our prayers…music to God's ears?

People at church were fond of saying, "This is God's house." Well, if it was, it seemed we had evicted Him.

Now that Sally had embraced Jesus, I was dating a religious fanatic.

We went to church because it was supposed to be good for us. Well, so was medicine, but we knew enough to take it more than once a week if we wanted to get better.

Don't get me wrong—she didn't look or act all that different. But I had learned about people like her while still in church. A fanatic was someone who tried to take God *outside* the church. A fanatic was someone who was glad to be with Him the other six days. A fanatic was someone who couldn't be totally happy until you were a fanatic too.

What I needed was a plan. I had to find some way to take her mind off Jesus and help focus it where it rightly belonged—on me. Eventually, a strategy blossomed that seemed foolproof. It was the H-bomb of diversions. The anthrax of countermeasures. One month after Sally made a lifetime commitment to Jesus, I asked her to make a lifetime commitment to me. The plan was "if you can't beat 'em, join 'em" and "divide and conquer" all rolled up in one.

A fanatic was someone who tried to take God outside the church. A fanatic was someone who was glad to be with Him the other six days. A fanatic was someone who couldn't be totally happy until you were a fanatic too.

Could Sally refuse me? Wasn't I the one who stuck by her through good times and bad? Hadn't I let her throw every shoe I owned at me one night when she was really mad at the world? As it turned out, she *couldn't* refuse. She said *yes!* and we set a date to be married six months later. Sally had only one request of me. "I need you to consider Jesus," she implored. "Consider Him as God. Consider Him as Lord. Just consider Him…please?"

I assured Sally I would consider the sovereignty of Jesus, but it was one of the most worthless promises I have ever made. I didn't set out to deceive her. I just figured I knew all there was to know and what I knew was that He was no friend of mine. People who followed Jesus ended up being hypocrites, or worse—

Republicans. I had a wedding to plan and yes, certainly, I was pre-pared to invoke God's name in the ceremony for the sake of mar-ital harmony, but that was about the extent of it.

We took an engagement class at the church Sally was attend-ing. The instructor gave us a compatibility test we figured we

> *People who fol-lowed Jesus ended up being hyp-ocrites, or worse— Republicans.*

would ace. But we never got the results. Between the time we tested and the day we would see how right we were for one another, Sally had a conversation with the teacher about being a couple divided by faith. He talked to her at length about being unequally yoked to someone who does not walk in faith with God. This was the hardest lesson on Sally's jour-ney toward truth, because it meant choosing between God and the man she loved. And she had known me two years longer!

Sally prayed for deliverance from the task ahead of her. But the more she petitioned God, the more she realized there was only one course of action. One evening she worked up enough courage and confronted me with Deuteronomy 22:10: "Do not plow with an ox and a donkey yoked together." As I didn't own any farmland, I said I was OK with that Scripture. She tried explaining what the passage meant. I wasn't sure if I was supposed to be the ox or the donkey, but I was on the verge of being offended. Suppose I am the ox in the story. That means I'm *engaged* to the donkey. Either way, I don't come out looking too good.

Sally told me she had no choice but to postpone our wed-ding until such time as I made a decision one way or another for Jesus. If I chose Jesus, we could be married. If I chose another path—she hoped we could always be friends. There was not an ounce of insincerity or coercion in what Sally shared. She was clearly broken over this decision. In the end, although I didn't understand why Jesus had to be an equal partner in our marriage,

I knew she believed it with all her heart. I didn't hold it against her.

Then she told me something I will always remember. She said, "But I'm not giving your ring back. I'm holding on to it. I don't want anyone else. I'll wait *ten years* if it takes you that long to make a decision."

Well.

That certainly got my attention. Valuing the truth as she did, I knew Sally wouldn't say something so extreme unless she really meant it. As the words poured out from her heart I had felt sure my head was on the chopping block. I had been given the ax by young ladies before. But this, most assuredly, was not the religious equivalent of "Let's be friends," which, of course, really means "I never want to see you again."

"OK," I offered. "I really will consider Jesus."

And I really did. But I took the slow road back. Along the way there were enough detours and road construction to drive us both crazy. I warned Sally, "Jesus has to be the truth for me too. I can't do this just for you."

"I wouldn't want it any other way," she whispered through tears.

I spent the next two years looking for—but mostly running from—God. It's funny. I spent all that time wrestling with God, but in the end it all came down to a ball, a bat, and a glove.

For quite a while, I thought Sally and I weren't going to make it. But never underestimate a good woman when the only weapon left in her arsenal is the indomitable power of prayer.

*Do not be yoked together
with unbelievers.
For what do righteousness and
wickedness have in common?
Or what fellowship can light have
with darkness?*
—2 Corinthians 6:14

Seventh-Inning Stretch

Selections from Sally Klein's Prayer Journal

January 16, 1985

Michael and I had a terrible scene Sunday about believing. And I was—still am a little—shell-shocked by the whole thing. I really do believe in God and the Bible—and Jesus (I'm still working on that). Not so much because I want to believe, although I suppose I must, to some degree, or I wouldn't. But more importantly, it is working in my life and making sense to me. And how on earth can I turn my back on something that seems to be the truth, or at least as close as I've ever gotten?

I am continually reminded I am disobeying God by agreeing to marry Michael in his unbelieving state. Yet what an insane pressure to put on someone—I won't marry Michael unless, or until, he believes. That can't be right either…. I pray for God's grace that Michael may come to grips with what he is and what he believes.

February 11, 1985

Michael and I are postponing our wedding. I finally broke my commitment to Michael and made my step of faith to God. The "ball" is now in God's court. I've signed and staked my life into God's hands. This is not easy—and yet somehow I know it's for the best, whatever happens. That is the only consolation—and it is NO CONSOLATION!!!!!

DO YOU HEAR ME, GOD?

I can't be angry, because I know it's right. But I am angry and hurt. I feel schizophrenic.

So, God, I've put the horse back in front of the cart. Forgive me, forgive Michael—Have mercy on us—don't sever us—heal us instead and make us whole—PLEASE!

April 2, 1985

I am praying every day for Michael—I think if it will happen God will have to break Michael's will—I feel the pressure has been brought to bear on Michael to make him face his life and convictions. God broke me with Michael. How He will break Michael I do not know. I can't believe God brought us together to tear us apart—to destroy the most wholesome thing in each other's lives. I have faith that our love is being tested—like steel or metal—and if we can bear it—we will never be apart.

May 5, 1985

Cinco de Mayo.

Today was the day Michael and I were going to be married. Today is the day I sacrificed to God. Today I could have had Michael. Now—I have God. God is with me always. That's what the Bible says. Yet I've spent much of my time with God praying for Michael, praying for me, praying for us. Today I am fasting.

The only visible chink in Michael's careful armor is his weight. There's a void he wants to fill—to ignore—and he's trying to satisfy it with food.

I satisfy his void some. But what he's really aching for is beyond me. That's why he can't get beyond a certain point in his diet. As the situation gets worse, Michael will probably get heavier—even though he seems calm on the outside—his weight is the yardstick for his pain. By his own words—Michael is seeking Love, as I sought and seek Truth. He has found a very strong human love with me, but even I can't give him all that he needs and wants. No one can—only God. God is Love—the ultimate, perfect Love—and Michael hurts because this is what he's seeking—but he hasn't found it.

The "mother" in me wants to do all this for him—and more—maybe that's partly why God stopped me. Maybe Michael too must put his faith in God first!

Lord, pierce his heart with your love and truth. Reach into the darkest corner of his soul, Lord—and make a miracle! Open his curtains—set your light in his heart so that he may see. Please Lord—for your sake, for your glory, for the triumph of light over dark—Save him! That he may glorify You.

Save us!

May 24, 1986

Fasting today until 6 p.m. Fasted all yesterday without a break—only water and tea. I'll not boast in myself here—for in myself I am nothing—but I prayed God would help me if this fast was a right and good thing in His eyes to do. I prayed for Michael—I always pray for Michael—he is my earthly treasure—he is the glass in whom I believe I sometimes see the Love of my Lord!

I do love the man, and, Lord, I thank You for the tenderness we have still for each other—and I beg You—I intercede for him, Lord, that you would move his heart—Change his heart from a heart of stone—to flesh—Make him SEE—Let him make that leap to salvation and Life in You, Jesus, help him!!!

And, Lord, I ask You for a sign—a way that we and especially I would know that it is your will that we marry each other—not just ours—But that truly Lord—You have called our hearts together. And Lord—if not—

Then I ask, Lord, that You would gently disengage our hearts each from the other—that we might not hurt so.

Lord—
I love him—
Help Me!
Help Him!
Help Us!

Under Your Mercy

June 16, 1986

I've put so much upon Michael—I guess I've really put his love before God. My biggest reason for praying to God is to inter-

cede for Michael—not to communicate with God—not to hear Him, but to tell Him my heart—instead of listening for His Word.

So afraid that God would take Michael away from me that I've been clutching and clinging to our love, building fences around it, so that even God couldn't get through.

And I've been jealous of everything that's usurped Michael's attention and focus away from his search for God. I have almost grown to hate baseball as a rival for God and for me—as the focus of much of Michael's time.

Lord—Forgive Me!

Teach me how to love You first! And then perhaps I will know how to love Michael better—more like You.

Father—help me let go of him—that he may seek You in his own way and time. Father, keep me from pushing and pulling at him as if he were a puppet—He's not! And help me remember— that as much as I love him—You love him more! Don't let him become hard in the ways of the world—but call his name, Lord, call his heart—that heart through which I've seen shades of your love—Call him, Lord—that he may know—You are the end of his quest—the only Love that will ever fill the hollow in his heart— the only Love—that will NEVER desert him! Heal him, Lord, and make him whole in You—

October 22, 1986

Lord—

I know You see around corners that I can't even guess at— but, Lord—like your Word in Hosea—"My heart turns within me." As You could never stop loving Israel—I love Michael.

Can I pray that You end this—NO!

Can I crucify my love for Michael—put it upon the altar,

even as Abraham did Isaac? If I must—Lord, You must show me how. Can I release Michael to You—knowing You love him more than any one can possibly fathom—Yes—every day, a little more—with your help!

Help me, Lord—

Show me how to love him the best way—your way!

"Ask and it will be given to you; seek and you will find; knock and the door will be opened to you."

—Matthew 7:7

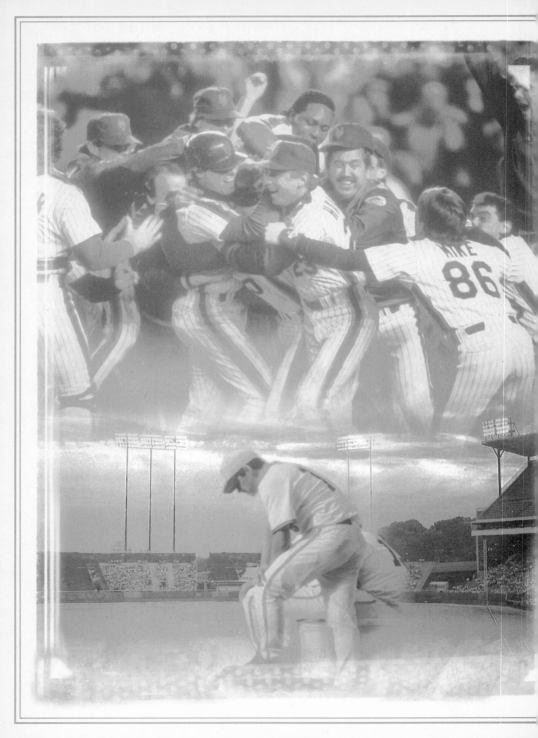

> *"God is a spectator, Scully.*
> *He just reads the box scores."*
>
> —*Agent Fox Mulder,* The X-Files

Bottom of the Seventh Inning

The Seventh Game—Part Two

I sat on the couch in my one-bedroom apartment, shifting restless feet from side to side. The World Series was on and the situation was tense. The telephone in the next room rang dimly, interrupting my solidarity with the game. If some rally-killing telemarketer thought I was leaving *this* game at *this* moment so he could tantalize me with the virtues of switching phone carriers—however clear the lines and wonderful the rate package—he was deeply, deeply, deeply delusional.

While Calvin Schiraldi had been pitching I was jackknifed forward, straining ever closer to the television, my caboose barely connected to the sofa's edge. A trained reader of body language would have quickly pegged me as someone who longed to be *inside* the TV—indeed, inside Shea Stadium where the New York crowd, dormant and resigned just moments ago, had begun to throw an impromptu Mardi Gras parade. The tide was turning.

Bob Stanley was now coming in from the Red Sox bullpen. He was taking over for Schiraldi, who had been unable to close the sale on Boston's first world championship since 1918. Still, the game, which hung by a thread, could be won by either team.

◆

With NBC cutting away for a commercial, I was given a few moments to digest what had happened so far in the delicious bottom of the tenth. After Wally Backman flied out to left field leading off the inning for the Mets, first baseman Keith Hernandez followed suit to center. With two down and no one on, Gary Carter coaxed a single to left off Schiraldi, staving off that quiet little death—the season's final pitch—for at least one batter longer. Down 5-3, Game Six, the Mets were still one out from elimination, and things were looking pretty grim.

While doctors were conferencing down the hall over whether or not to pull the plug, the Mets clung to life support like a homeless man to his shopping cart. They were dogged, these New Yorkers, and never more so than when pinch hitter Kevin Mitchell slapped the second hit of the inning and found himself on first base, the potential tying run. The comatose patient was suddenly showing signs of life. Sox fans everywhere began fearing the Mets might actually be exhibiting a pulse.

With two runners on, Ray Knight worked Schiraldi to an 0-2 count. Now he had the pitcher right where he wanted him. Knight flicked his bat, connecting on a lazy fly ball that looked to end the game. Miraculously, however, the ball eluded the second baseman. Carter came around to score, and the game was now 5-4. Physicians removed the respirator, and the patient, coughing and wheezing, began breathing on his own. Night over for Schiraldi.

◆

Bob Stanley finished his warm-ups. The couch could no longer contain me. As I leaned forward, the laws of physics subpoenaed my body painfully to the living room floor. Fine by me. If you can't sit in a sky box, field level is the next best thing.

Stanley was again looking in for his sign. The count on Mookie Wilson was even—two balls and two strikes. Kevin Mitchell danced off third base. Wilson's heart was pirouetting in his chest. Adrenaline like a Texas gusher was pumping through my veins. The veteran reliever leaned back, reared up, and fired a bullet that missed its target, skipping all the way back to the screen. A wild pitch! Mitchell raced home with the tying run, with Knight advancing to second. Trembling, I returned to the couch.

I began to think this breathless contest was maybe the greatest game I'd ever seen—or at least the most exciting comeback. So much was at stake. So many dreams on the line.

I wished Sally was with me to share the moment. To this day I can't believe an avid Red Sox fan like Sally didn't come over to watch her team win baseball's ultimate prize. I do know there was an empty seat beside me and a void in my heart.

Eighteen months had passed since Sally had called off our marriage. As broken engagements go, the fact that we kept dating each other exclusively made it one of the more unusual breakups on record. Just three months prior to ending the engagement, she had committed her life to God. She biblically, spiritually, and personally felt the need for a similar commitment from me.

"Right now we have love," she reasoned, "and that's good and beautiful. But there was a time when our parents must have loved each other just as much as we do…yet it wasn't enough." She was crying and, of course, was referring to my folks, who were divorced, and to her parents, who were permanently separated. "You and I bring so much baggage, so much brokenness to this relationship. There's no way we can survive unless we both ask God into our marriage."

I felt as though she was holding a gun to my head. In fact, I had told her that very thing recently during what became one of our biggest arguments. I don't like ultimatums, and I work overtime to avoid conflict. But the real truth, when you come right down to it, is that I've never been very comfortable looking in the mirror. Life can be so much easier without the messy complication of self-examination.

I suppose there are events or issues in just about everyone's existence they would rather set behind them permanently—even if it means sweeping an elephant under the carpet. But whenever you do that, invariably some well-meaning, misguided Samaritan gently comments on the lump beneath your rug.

> *The real truth, when you come right down to it, is that I've never been very comfortable looking in the mirror. Life can be so much easier without the messy complication of self-examination.*

"What lump?" you ask defensively, straddling the bulging carpet while trying to involve her in a card trick.

"A huge, pachyderm-sized lump," the Samaritan replies. Then she asks if you wouldn't just like to lift up the rug and get rid of whatever is making those peanut-crunching sounds.

"Thanks," you reply tersely, now tap-dancing the entire choreography of *Swan Lake* to cover the gratuitous munching, "but isn't there a Galatian or Corinthian who needs you right now?"

Almost two years, and I was no closer to examining my heart than on the day Sally placed us on hold. What was wrong with me? Was it pride or something else that allowed me to keep my Creator at arm's length?

Sure, I believed God existed. Believed He gave me life.

Believed in the deity of Jesus. Believed, even, in the Holy Spirit and the Virgin Birth—all foundational elements of the Christian faith. But I had grown weary of the hypocrisy I had seen in the church of my youth. I didn't want to commit to that set of ten rules again—even though I was pretty sure they were righteous and holy. I had serious doubts I could keep them in any real and honorable way.

Or so I kept telling myself.

So after Sally and I had the blowup, I set aside my pride and asked God to reveal himself to me—to close the sale on a pitch I had heard many times, but always from the mouth of an agent. This time I needed to hear from the Seller himself.

"Show me, God," I prayed. "Show me who You really are and why I'm so stubborn as to refuse You entry into my life. Overcome my hurdles—please! Show me the things that prevent me from calling your name like a long-lost friend. Then steal them from my heart. Show me, God. Show me."

◆

Mookie Wilson was hanging in there. After the wild pitch, he'd fouled the next one off. How could anyone cope with this kind of strain? I was now in full cardiac arrest despite being nearly a continent removed from the pressure.

Stanley gripped the ball in his glove and glanced over his shoulder at Knight leading off second. He whirled quickly and fired a strike to the catcher Gedman—but again Wilson got a piece of it.

I couldn't move. My mind, heart, and eyes were riveted, my central nervous system gridlocked. No use dialing 9-1-1. Paramedics were answering calls like this all over the country. Something inside was either going to collapse or snap or blow or hemorrhage, and I would become a footnote in the annals of baseball history.

Dear God, please *don't let Bob Stanley throw another pitch!*

Please *won't you make both teams run out on the field, wrap their arms around one another, and declare this thing a tie?*

Anyone who tells you God doesn't answer prayer has no idea what he's talking about.

◆

Did God respond to your passionate plea on that fateful day?
Yes.

Did God keep Mr. Stanley from throwing another pitch to Mr. Wilson?
No.

Did God somehow intervene in Game Six of the 1986 World Series?
It's entirely possible.

Did God allow the game—and then the Series—to end in a tie?
Are you *nuts*? This is baseball, not hockey!

◆

On October 25, 1986, God did indeed answer my prayer. Only it wasn't the please-give-Bob-Stanley-a-hamstring-pull-so-I-won't-have-a-stroke prayer. Instead, He responded that day to my petition from several weeks prior. I had asked Him some time earlier to reveal whatever remained a stumbling block between Him and me, that it might be removed from my path forever.

He reminded me of a young woman I'd met back in college. Her name was Linda, and there was a time when I would have given anything for her love. We were introduced through some mutual friends in the

> *Something inside was either going to collapse or snap or blow or hemorrhage, and I would become a footnote in the annals of baseball history.*

late 1970s. She was sweet and beautiful in a Roma Downey *Touched-by-an-Angel* kind of way. When her shy smile hit me broadside I could scarcely contain my good fortune.

There was a quality of goodness and purity about Linda that was at once refreshing and compelling. As we were becoming friends, I learned she was a born-again Christian. We started dating a little. Occasionally I would accompany her to church. Her pastor shared powerful, thought-provoking messages. His gift for imparting the Word of God was stirring the ashes of faith within my heart. One day, despite years of religious misgivings, I accepted Jesus as my Lord and Savior. Later that year I was baptized in the American River.

But as things began taking off in my relationship with God, Linda's feelings for me began solidifying more into the realm of friendship than love. I was young and foolish and wrote desperate, painful letters that only served, I'm sure, to help her see she had made the right decision.

Brokenhearted, I continued going to church. It was a large congregation comprised mainly of baby boomers, and everywhere I looked there were couples holding hands, couples in love, individuals who had someone special with whom to share their walk with God. I felt conspicuous in my singleness, like the last dinosaur in a new world order of humans.

So I did the only rational thing a young man in denial could do in such a situation. I got mad at God and blamed everything on Him. "Why did You take her away from me?" I railed. Friends tried to counsel me about God's mercy and love for me. I wanted no part of their platitudes. I just wanted to stop hurting.

Since church was a place that reminded me of Linda, and something as basic as opening the Bible peeled back my flesh and exposed the sheer rawness of my heart, I felt I had little choice. In the interest of self-preservation I just walked away without looking back. I never renounced God. I simply didn't want to think about Him anymore.

My decision to follow Jesus had been real and sincere. I had not answered an altar call to win a fair maiden's hand. But like the parable Jesus told, I had built the foundation of my faith upon the sand of a woman's love rather than on the solid rock of God's Word. So when the first storm hit, everything I had placed upon that shaky ground washed away with the tide.

This is the roadblock God showed me. The issues I had about church while growing up were completely valid concerns that had impeded my progress in learning to know and follow God. In hindsight, I should never have allowed the foolishness of man to keep me from the righteousness of God. While accurate in its detail, the story I shared about my early church days was a smoke screen—a less painful way to deal with my separation from God. My position on my estrangement from Sally was a crock—and I was a fraud.

This was the history lesson God revealed in answer to my prayer. But why did He choose *this* moment to make His point, with the 1986 baseball season hanging precariously in the balance?

◆

Where were you when JFK was shot?

At Pioneer Elementary School. My third grade teacher, Mrs. Eva, told us the president had been assassinated.

Where were you when you first heard Elvis was dead?

Soaping up in the shower, listening to music on the radio when a breaking news bulletin stopped the music.

Where were you when Mookie Wilson hit the ground ball to first?

Where *was* I? I was out of my mind—*that's* where I was!

◆

His at-bat in the bottom of the tenth of the sixth game of the 1986 World Series had been going on so long that Mookie Wilson's player's-union pension had kicked in sometime around the middle of it. Since last setting foot in the Mets dugout, three presidential elections had been held and the word "bad" still had only negative connotations. Seven pitches that lasted a lifetime. And then pitch number eight came bearing down.

Routine was the only label you could give it. There was nothing special or particularly difficult about the ordinary grounder heading straight for Sox first baseman Bill Buckner, several feet off the bag. It was neither a rocket he would dive for nor a soft roller Buckner needed to charge. Ray Knight was running toward third, but his heart couldn't have been in it.

In hindsight, I should never have allowed the foolishness of man to keep me from the righteousness of God.

Buckner was going to field the ball and either take it to first himself or toss it to Stanley covering the bag. The game would continue into the next inning tied 5-5.

But a funny thing happened on the way to the eleventh.

That routine grounder to first turned into a routine roller to right. The ball, a skipping stone across the infield pond of Shea, must have hit a dead spot on a lily pad as Buckner had anticipated one more ever-so-slight bounce that never came. Had Wilson been playing croquet, he couldn't have split the wickets of Buckner's leg span with any more accuracy or aplomb.

Knight galloped home like a modern-day Paul Revere delivering the news of a New York miracle more powerful than the one that happened on 34th Street. The Mets celebrated jubilantly. Boston walked off the field stunned. I couldn't move. "Un be leave a bull," were the five words threatening to cross my lips. But I couldn't *talk* either.

After two men were retired, the Mets had taken three hits, a wild pitch, and a mundane ground ball, tossed them into a blender, and poured out the most improbable comeback in World Series history—final score: New York 6, Boston 5.

I neither wept nor celebrated, for my mind was all but immersed in some *Outer Limits*-type interplay that had begun way back when Gary Carter kept the game alive with the inning's first hit. Carter was standing on first, probably relieved he had not made the final out of the World Series.

It is important to understand that what I share next is neither exaggeration nor hyperbole. I love having fun with words, and if the imprint of truth has found its way onto a flattened wad of Silly Putty, I have no problem at all stretching it this way or that, pulling on the playful substance for a tongue-in-cheek distortion of reality. I do this if it's clear the contortion of facts is for the purpose of whimsy or satire, but never to lend a story more importance than it has earned.

As the camera showed Carter taking his lead off first, the television set I was watching—that seventy-five-dollar Magnavox special I picked up at the Salvation Army store—appeared to flash maybe two feet closer to me. One moment it was ten feet away, the next it seemed as if it was eight. And the screen got larger, expanding from twenty-two inches to perhaps a twenty-four inch model. I know it sounds fantastic. I know it sounds like a lie. I didn't believe it either, shaking my head and trying to blink the set back into the corner. But it stayed eight feet away until Kevin Mitchell got his single. Then the TV appeared as if it was six feet away and the screen grew larger still.

Had I been a drinking man, the explanation would have been apparent. Yet having never touched a mind-altering substance in my life, I was unable to rationalize this as a seventies drug flashback.

This was the point where a chuckling Alan Funt was supposed to come out to shake my hand and point to the hidden camera in the bookcase. But Alan missed his entrance as Knight dropped the ball into right-center. Unfortunately, the television picked up *its* cue as it once more appeared two feet closer, a couple inches larger. The panic I described earlier was setting in.

I wanted to get out of the room, but I was mesmerized by the game. I didn't move because I couldn't bear to miss what came next. This, by the way, is the ultimate definition of a baseball fanatic. A television is chasing him, but he's adjusting the color-contrast knobs to get a better representation of the game as the aggressive picture tube backs him down a flight of stairs.

Why was this happening? What did it mean? Who—or what—was behind my apparent hallucinations?

Something occurred to me as Bob Stanley threw the ball away, the tying run scored, and everyone moved up—including the TV. As bizarre as this sounds, it began to feel as if the improbable events of the game were being played out entirely for my benefit. Now, I have a fairly healthy ego, but as C. S. Lewis was fond of describing Jesus, He was *not* a good man and a wise teacher. He was either who he said He was—the Son of God—or He was a diabolical liar or a stark raving lunatic. In the same sense, this late rally was either playing out on my behalf, or I am the greatest megalomaniac in recorded history. Of course, only a true megalomaniac would think he had the greatest ego of all time.

The ball skipped through Bill Buckner's legs, the Mets were climbing all over one another, and the TV was practically in my face. This was not funny. This was Rod Serling meets Pee Wee Herman. I followed the replays of Wilson's grounder to Buckner, and something hit me with the clarity a two-by-four can occasionally bring to the forehead.

God apparently had done this for me. He had arranged this moment because He loved me. He had used a World Series game because it was the surest way to reach a baseball fanatic. He wanted my attention because…because…

Come to think of it, why *did* He want my attention? Was it because of Sally? She had been interceding for me through the veil of a broken heart. God knew I had been allowing this beautiful woman to swing in the breeze as my indifference to Him continued. Was it Sally's faithful prayer that brought God to this room to confront me—or was it my own?

Had God changed the course of a World Series just for me...or had He simply known what was coming and used it to gain my attention?

When most people reflect back on Game Six, they think the Mets won the World Series that night. In fact, New York only tied it up, forcing a seventh and deciding game. As I continued trying to analyze God's motivation for using the Series to reach me, I wondered if there might be a clue somewhere along the path both the Sox and Mets had taken to get there.

Two teams battle their way through a 162-game schedule. After winning two tiers of playoffs, which involved up to twelve extra games, the best of the best meet in a modernized coliseum. The stronger team battles the weaker into submission. The arena is a best-of-seven play-off, with the first team to win four games the victor.

Had God changed the course of a World Series just for me...or had He simply known what was coming and used it to gain my attention?

In this Series, both teams had proved, thus far, evenly matched. Each had secured three victories. Each tasted the same number of defeats. This lifted the two proud warriors above the rabble to a mountaintop experience dreamed by many, realized by few—the seventh game.

The seventh game is sudden death. The moment of reckoning. Judgment Day. One team would win and have its name written in the minds and hearts of millions. The other would lose, slipping into the shadows of faded memory like a silent film star in the Technicolor era.

Most every baseball fan knows that in 1960 Bill Mazeroski hit a seventh-game, ninth-inning home run for the Pirates to win their first world championship since 1925. But do people remember who lost that World Series? Usually not. We are a culture that celebrates the conquerors and reviles the vanquished.

I began to examine my life in terms of winning and losing. In a manner of speaking, I, too, was facing my own personal seventh game. In terms of eternity, I had been risking much sitting up on that fence for so long. I looked down on one side and saw Jesus. He was playing with children in a field of high, flowing grass. Everything on that side was filled with light and God's goodness. The other side was enveloped in shadow. Nothing even growing there except a bunch of weeds.

I realized I should make a decision—if only to release Sally from her promise to stand by me. Remain where I was or come down off the fence—these were my choices. I had asked God to show me the way to bridge the chasm that lay between us. Hadn't He done that?

I was waffling badly and knew it. Something was about to give. In one final, magnificent burst of defiance, I cried out silently the question that my heart had never reconciled: "Why did you do it, God? Why did you take Linda away from me?"

His answer resonated like a violin bow moving tenderly across the strings of my heart. *Because I had something even better for you.*

I once heard a pastor say that if you were working on a decision for God and you had five reasons for

> *I realized I should make a decision—if only to release Sally from her promise to stand by me. Remain where I was or come down off the fence—these were my choices.*

following Him and five against, sometimes you just had to take a leap of faith. As I looked over at the side of the fence without God, I realized there was one thing I knew for sure. I did not want to be in the dark anymore.

So it was that on the night the Mets and Red Sox had reached their point of decision, I jumped off the fence and asked God to forgive this prodigal son for turning his back on his Father. I embraced Him as my Savior and received His grace in full.

The next morning, in the wee early hours near dawn, unable to contain myself in sleep, I sat down and wrote a lyric about my experience the previous night. Baseball was the backdrop for my song about making the most important decision of my life. Stubborn to the end, I waited two weeks before sharing the news. I guess I just wanted to be doubly sure the Jesus vaccine in my heart "took" before I invited Sally over and read her the words.

◆

November 23, 1986

Michael asked Jesus into his life. We spent the whole day together. He read me a lyric he wrote called "The Seventh Game." Needless to say—I cried.

God is ever faithful.

God's mercy endures forever!!!

Michael proposed again.

◆

The Seventh Game

You've had quite a season and you're almost at the top
With a dream that touched a million smiling faces
But today is gonna be your biggest challenge yet
Better make sure that you're touching all the bases—'cause

This time you're playing for all the marbles
This time you can't afford to lose
There's a time to run and play
And a time to run away
Eventually there comes a time to choose
One Name
So what are you gonna do
When the season
Comes down to the seventh game

It's been quite a struggle as you try to do your best
But every day it seems you're losing ground
You're swinging for the fences with a toothpick, kid
When a sacrifice could turn this game around—'cause

This time you're playing for all the marbles
This time you can't afford to lose
There's a time to run and play
And a time to run away
Eventually there comes a time to choose
One Name
So what are you gonna do
When the Series
Comes down to the seventh game

Now you can see what you're made of
When your back's against the wall
The score is even, now just believe and
You can win it all—'cause

This time you're playing for all the marbles
This time you can't afford to lose
There's a time to run and play
And a time to run away

Eventually there comes a time to choose
One Name
So what are you gonna do
When your whole life
Comes down to the seventh game

Yeah what are you gonna say
When the Spirit comes to play
The seventh game

Every boy builds a shrine to some baseball hero,
and before that shrine a candle always burns.

—Judge Kenesaw Mountain Landis

I don't know if I'm making a mistake,
but I'm raising my kid as a Giant fan.

—Toots Shor

Eighth Inning

When a Hero Falls

When hotel security finally broke down the door, they found him crumpled on the floor, lying in a pool of his own blood. There had been a history of heart problems and that, apparently, was what felled this stately redwood of a man.

The blood, a product of the fall, was from his nose, and it stained the carpet near his motionless right arm. It was a limb that had brought him great fame and distinction. It was an arm that had not thrown a major-league pitch in twenty-four years.

Funny thing about life. At thirty-two he was too old to pitch. But at fifty-six, Don Drysdale was far too young to die.

The Los Angeles Dodgers were in Montreal to take on the Expos. I was watching the game in progress when announcer Vin Scully shared the grim news with a few million viewers—and me.

The message was almost surreal, too unbelievable to be consumed at one sitting. Dodger Hall-of-Famer and long-time broadcaster Drysdale was committed to the ages. But how could he be gone? Wasn't it only yesterday I had seen Don interview Eric Karros on the postgame show? Wasn't it, indeed, only yesterday I had seen Drysdale outduel Juan Marichal on a wind-beaten summer's afternoon at Candlestick Park?

♦

It would be easy for one to assume, since I live in Los Angeles and my passion for baseball is above reproach, that I must naturally be a Dodger fan. This assumption would not only be erroneous, but could seriously undermine the possibility of any meaningful friendship between one and I.

A native son of Sacramento, I was raised about one hundred miles from the San Francisco Bay Area. I am an unabashedly dyed-in-the-wool paid-my-dues-and-sung-dem-blues-trade-our-stars-for-old-used-cars-tried-our-best-here-wait-'til-next-year-DH-hatin'-pennant-waitin'-miss-you-Willie-'Stick's-too-chilly-bleacher-bums-with-Dad-and-Grandpa-praise-the-Lord-we're-not-in-Tampa lifelong San Francisco Giants fan.

> *Funny thing about life. At thirty-two he was too old to pitch. But, at fifty-six, Don Drysdale was far too young to die.*

To the surprise of my bride, I mentioned the team in my wedding vows—and lived to see the honeymoon. I came dangerously close to naming my first daughter Wilimina Mays O'Connor. Need an Etch-A-Sketch? Is this the portrait of a rational human, let alone a Dodger lover?

Of course, with Official Fanhood comes the unwritten company policy: Love the Giants, hate the Dodgers. It's a crude but inspiring credo. Why can't the tax code be this uncomplicated?

I once witnessed two extremely foolish young men holding a homemade "Go Dodgers!!!!!" banner scrawled on a bed sheet, parading around the entire upper deck at Candlestick. This was shocking to me, because at the time I didn't know Dodger fans could write. A wave of dangerous-sounding boos followed them from section to section. It grew so loud some of the players popped their heads up from the dugout.

As the duo approached our section, the booing reached a crescendo. Five immensely large young men, perhaps fraternity brothers, decided to employ a coda—their own special brand of improvised, hairy-armed conducting—designed to bring this symphony of derision to a swift and merciful conclusion. The two geniuses with the Magic Markers and linen were unceremoniously dragged into a nearby tunnel. The stadium faithful held its collective breath. Five minutes later the five wise guys emerged, ripping the confiscated bed sheet into a hundred beautiful pieces and scattering them to the wind. Pandemonium ensued. Grown men wept.

This was the first and only hate crime I have ever witnessed. It is also the only one I have ever stood for and applauded.

◆

*"What do you do when a hero falls
and doesn't get up?"*

The question appeared from nowhere, then swirled around in my head like a hot dog wrapper at Wrigley Field, never quite landing on one answer before kicking up again and taking off to examine the next.

I spent the following week in a bit of a funk. To tell the truth, I didn't exactly know why. Why was this deceased baseball player lately preoccupying my thoughts and highlighting old clippings in the scrapbook of my heart? Sure, a hero had fallen, but he wasn't *my* hero.

My boyhood heroes were fellows named Mays, McCovey, Marichal, Cepeda, Haller, Hart, and Alou. Together we would set upon a quest each April to defeat the dreaded Angelenos for rights to the coveted National League Grail. Often I would smuggle my transistor radio into class or under the bedcovers for fleeting audio glimpses of their timeless, bloodless battles.

This was the first and only hate crime I have ever witnessed. It is also the only one I have ever stood for and applauded.

And fierce they were, usually boiling down to the final weekend of the campaign. Inevitably, when the dust had settled, it was Sir Wills, Sir Parker, Sir Koufax, and Sir Drysdale who were left clinching the cup of victory. It was, just as inevitably, those gallant but vanquished Giants who were relegated to long cold winters licking their wounds and plotting new strategies to the tune of "Wait 'til Next Year."

But Drysdale was the glue—the heart and spirit of those Dodger teams. As a pitcher he was remarkable. As a competitor he was devastating. Without him I might have seen the team of my youth appear in as many World Series as the legendary Yankees. He was Joker to my Batman, Moriarty to my Holmes. He was never my enemy, but ever my nemesis.

In his prime he was a slayer of dreams and an executioner of hope. He was the most effective Giant-killer since David. I hated him for the uniform he wore, yet if I am to be completely honest, I now realize I also loved him for the skill and valor he displayed while wearing it. I suppose this, above all, is the confusing paradox that plagued me in the days following Drysdale's death.

"What do you do when a hero falls and doesn't get up?"

I began to realize that this question, which I had largely considered rhetorical, must have had a deeper purpose than the intrusion on my existence of a week-long walk down memory lane. Apparently, for this thought to stop nagging me, I was going to have to meet it head on. Either that or watch that baseball movie again to see how the guy in *Field of Dreams* dealt with *his* disembodied voice.

Clearly there was something here I was not eager to face. So I went to my study. Standing amid countless volumes of bound wisdom, I reached the shelf that often draws me in times of worry and distress. There, on its side, lay the source of all truth that passes understanding. Expectantly, I opened the fortune cookie: "He who looks to man for heroics invests himself in a perishable commodity."

The words hit me with the weight of a Sumo wrestler in a death grip with his twin. As perishable commodities go, the cookie wasn't bad either.

You see, I still want to cling to a crazy notion that Willie Mays loves and cares for the twelve-year-old boy I grew out of, and that he'll hit the home run that wins the Series and forever we'll be best buddies, Willie and me. But the truth is that Mays is an aging icon who probably couldn't care less about the boys who spent their youth on him and wouldn't even sign my baseball if I didn't plunk down a hundred dollars for the privilege.

> *In his prime he was a slayer of dreams and an executioner of hope. He was the most effective Giant-killer since David.*

The bottom line is that it may take a day, a week, a year, or decades, but eventually the object of your adulation will fall down and not get back up. Maybe he won't pay his taxes, trading pinstripes for pen-stripes. Maybe he'll throw a lit firecracker into a crowd and later claim it was just a joke. Maybe he'll gamble on baseball and deny it ever happened. Or maybe, committing the ultimate hero's sin, he'll just grow old and die.

And when he does, you'll be left with a lot of square-peg questions trying to fill a round-hole void in your heart.

Many are the heroes who have fallen. But, incredibly, there is only One who has ever gotten back up. As much as we choose to admire the Ruths, the Mantles, the Drysdales of this world, this much is inescapable: What they have accomplished, while special in its own context, will wither and die like the grass of the field. Yet the unblemished record of Jesus Christ, His achievements, and His love for His children will last beyond any mortal Hall of Fame we may ever create.

When I look in the mirror and ask myself the question, "What did Willie Mays ever do for you?" I'd like to say he made me the man I am today. That he helped to shape my character, built up my confidence, offered sage advice in crisis intervals, and made sure there were a couple of bucks in the old bank account for my college education.

Many are the heroes who have fallen. But, incredibly, there is only One who has ever gotten back up.

That's what I'd *like* to say. But the truth is, short of administering a couple hundred vicarious thrills to a hero-starved kid, Willie never lifted a finger for me. He never knew I existed. Still, I worshiped on his altar.

Jesus, on the other hand, gave me His *life* that I might have, among other things, the freedom to choose my heroes. I'm ashamed to say which guy owns more real estate on my bookshelf.

Why is it, then, I find it so delicious to give myself in wild, spontaneous, rapturous applause to some self-centered, over-paid athlete who just slugged a game-winning homer into the upper deck when it is still difficult to lose myself in the sweetness of a worship service? Why does gravity tug so at these hands designed by God to be lifted wholeheartedly in praise, when, in moments not nearly so regal, they are generously filled with helium?

So simple is the answer, not even a fortune cookie is necessary. I guess I'm scared. Sometimes I still cannot fathom returning, in a healthy way, a love so pure and unconditional as the one God offers to each of us. It's a frightening enough prospect to send me and other middle-aged boys scurrying to the stands in search of false, but safer, gods.

I love the Lord but, you see, I've got rules and conditions. I've got parameters and calibrated defenses. I've got excuses and detailed explanations. I've got...I've got...I've got to grow up...and into the man...the *son*...He intended me to be from the beginning.

Does this mean I shouldn't ever go to a baseball game and let loose with the occasional lung-clearing cheer for my team or player of choice? Not at all. So long as I am able to enjoy the excellence I see down on the field and recognize it as a momentary diversion from life's struggles. So long as we remember the true struggles are the spiritual battles waged

Why is it that I find it so delicious to give myself in wild, spontaneous, rapturous applause to some self-centered, over-paid athlete who just slugged a game-winning homer into the upper deck when it is still difficult to lose myself in the sweetness of a worship service?

daily in our hearts and minds, and that the outcome of this warfare will ultimately decide to whom we offer our adulation and for whom we have nothing left but a place on the trash heap with the banana peels and the day-old box scores.

So what do you do when a hero falls and doesn't get up? You thank him for the memories. You thank him for reminding you of the difference between what is eternal and what is temporal. And you try to hang on to that the next time some golden-boy phenom tosses fifty-eight consecutive scoreless innings and you start to give your heart away so cheaply again.

"To whom will you compare me?
Or who is my equal?" says
the Holy One.
Lift your eyes and look to
the heavens:
Who created all these?
He who brings out the starry host
one by one.
—Isaiah 40:25-26

Ninth Inning

The Voice of God

How do you hear God? In the breeze of a cool summer evening? In the dew of a morning so cold and beautiful it makes you ache with pleasure? Do you hear Him in a book, a child's laugh, an exquisite piece of music? Is the voice audible? Do you hear it in the moment when your breathing is still and the only noise is a cricket serenading the universe? Or is the voice of God something intangible, a sense, a feeling, a gut-level message delivered like a silent email to the soul? Are God's attempts at direct communication real and alive with the promise of holy touch, or merely the wishful thinking of an overactive, deity-starved imagination?

Henry Blackaby, theologian and coauthor of the popular Bible study program *Experiencing God*, explains his view of how God chooses to communicate with us: "God speaks by the Holy Spirit through the Bible, prayer, circumstances, and the church to reveal himself, His purposes, and His ways."

I believe God has revealed himself to me in each of the ways suggested by Blackaby. That's right—the same God who took six days to create the earth, the God of Abraham, Isaac, and Jacob—this God has generously shared an eternal wisdom from His heart to mine on several occasions. Not because I am special or gifted have I received this blessing, but simply because I am His. At these times I have alternately listened intently, been oblivious, followed instructions faithfully, or ignored directives and loving suggestions and chosen to follow my own path.

Are God's attempts at direct communication real and alive with the promise of holy touch, or merely the wishful thinking of an overactive, deity-starved imagination?

Still, God is faithful, even persistent. Often I wonder why. With all His infinite power, His vast universal access to any of the great minds or souls in the history of our planet, why would He choose to single *me* out for a conversation? It doesn't make sense. Why would the King reach out to befriend a pawn? Why would He keep pursuing me until we have that talk? We know daddies sit down with their children, share their joys and sorrows, give counsel, take time to listen to their hearts. But God has billions of kids. I have *two* and it's hard to find the time!

When Sally wants to hear from God, she heads for the regal cliffs at Zuma Beach in Southern California. Maybe it's the wind whipping her hair around her shoulders as she spreads a blanket on a dune. Maybe it's the spray in her face or the sand between her toes that calls her into proximity with her Father. Or maybe she leaves the beach and begins the ascent to her special place because the cliffs offer a towering, unobstructed channel between her and her Lord. And she wants nothing to come between them.

I know what she is feeling when she takes in Zuma. I, too, have a special place where I have only to inhale and nature generously fills my lungs with the heady stuff of creation. I climb the concrete steps to the back wall of a stadium, shuffle sideways down a long, empty row, and plop myself down into a powder-blue hard-plastic seat, or maybe a green, splintered bench desperate for repainting.

At that moment I am not simply perched in a remote section in the upper deck at Dodger Stadium or the distant bleachers of an obscure Little League park. I am getting ready to be with God.

We have a date. I know He will show up.

So today I am balancing a condiment-loaded hot dog in one hand while reaching for a fresh, but nearly flat, twenty-four-ounce Diet Coke with the other. I am drinking in the great green expanse that lies between majestic yellow foul poles, resting like pencils in two monstrous holders. If you look up the term "great outdoors" in the newly expanded *O'Connor, Funk, & Wagnalls Encyclopedia*, this is definitely the picture you see.

No kidding. This is where I come to consider life's problems and answers. This is where I dream of tomorrow—where I ponder faults and virtues of the universe and become extremely introspective. Baseball and its fields give me ample motive and opportunity for review and projection.

A lot of folks these days say baseball is too slow and boring. Ten minutes of action packed into three and a half hours. They are missing the point.

Bill Veeck knew what the clock watchers simply cannot or will not grasp. "Baseball," he preached, "is a game to be savored rather than taken in gulps." He understood that as a fine wine needs to breathe, a baseball game requires space and patience to experience maximum possible enjoyment and understanding.

Of course, there have been days I've shown up at the

ballpark with my friends in a rowdy, take-no-prisoners mood. Such days demand that fun be had, and that is as it should be. But some days are meant for serious reflection.

So you find a seat up and away from the masses. You arrive alone unless you are with someone who understands why you have come. You are now blending with the colors on nature's palette. These ballpark oils and pastels are no less beautiful than any redwood you will one day sit beneath, attempting to feel one with. You are awed and silent as in a cathedral. The first pitch is thrown and you enter into worship. God is as difficult to find here as a politician in an even-numbered year.

> *A lot of folks these days say baseball is too slow and boring. Ten minutes of action packed into three and a half hours. They are missing the point.*

He is on the field as the wonderful displays of athletic excellence invigorate our senses. He is in the dugout as that most generous of gifts, the human mind, churns out a strategy to slay the opposing army. And then, when you least expect it, God is quite simply in the next seat, leaning back, laughing, and cheering alongside you.

As any fan this day who cleared his schedule, bought a ticket, and paid for parking, God is rooting. But when you lean over and ask Him which team he is hoping will win…He surprises you. For He is not at all rooting in the traditional sense, with one eye on a favorite team or beloved player and another against the behemoth blocking that team's path to the play-offs and World Series.

He is rooting for *everyone.*

He wants the batter to hit a homer, and He wants the pitcher to strike Home Run Harry out. He wants the shortstop to field the sharp grounder cleanly and the runner to leg out the infield single. He wants the third base coach to judge flawlessly whether his runner can score from second on a single to center, the catcher to hang onto the second baseman's relay, and the umpire to get the call right when the dust settles at home. God wants the peanut vendor to have an exceptional sales day and the scoreboard operator to execute his cues with precision timing.

God is rooting for everyone.

Sure, He knows they can't all succeed. He knows there will be errors. He knows someone has to lose. Heck, He even knows *who* will lose before the game starts. He was in possession of this information before the first baseball was formed on the eighth day.

But these are His kids. Picture yourself a dad or mom at a Little League game with a son pitching and your daughter at bat. Who do you root for? How do you not pull for both of them?

On this day, it seems, He is also rooting for me.

He reminds me of a men's retreat I attended a few years back with some guys from my church. *Do you remember?* He prods, savoring a bite from an ice cream sandwich that seems to be delivering particular enjoyment. *Do you remember what I showed you on that day?*

I do. I do remember the glimpse of a legacy my heavenly Father gave me one Saturday in May 1996. It had been terribly meaningful at the time but had somehow gotten stashed up in the attic, lodged between a faint recollection of an eleven-year-old getting caught stealing comic books at a local drugstore and a high school sophomore's memory of his awkward first date.

I dust off the keepsake and carry it downstairs into the light. Why had I exiled this treasure anyway? Oh yeah…because it was as painful as it was beautiful. Something about confronting a serious weight issue—and myself in the process. After a while it was no longer comfortable to face the lesson or the Teacher. So both were dispatched to a distant corner of my mind to collect dust and cobwebs like an unwanted present the day after Christmas.

And now God was asking me, amid the peace and solitude of

my 38,540 closest friends, to revisit the memory for reasons I could not discern but found highly suspicious.

But hey, how do you say no when God is buying the Cracker Jack?

I had always avoided church men's retreats religiously. I think part of it had to do with the fact that I feel more complete and, yes, safer, with Sally by my side. I'm sure there were some fear-of-intimacy issues also. Specifically, male bonding—which, in my opinion, cannot be done really well without a television set, a sports event, and a generous supply of Krazy Glue.

Fortunately there would be plenty of Ping-Pong, foosball, hoops, hiking, and swimming to distract us from the temptation of too many touchy-feely Kodak moments. Then, too, there was softball on the schedule.

Ah, slow-pitch softball—the illegitimate stepchild of baseball. That pseudo sport of pot-bellied kings who relive their wasted youth and scattered, windblown dreams by swinging a stick at a ball so large and sluggish that you couldn't miss if you were blindfolded, holding a salami sandwich in one hand and a bottle of Yoo-hoo in the other.

Male bonding, in my opinion, cannot be done really well without a television set, a sports event, and a generous supply of Krazy Glue.

This, by the way, is my preferred batting stance.

I once saw somebody swing and miss in a slow-pitch game, but he had time to regroup and take another cut just before the ball finished crossing the plate. It was a lovely three-run homer that won the game.

I used to love playing baseball as a kid. But as I grew older most of the leagues where adults still played hardball were also paying them millions of dollars to do it. So I latched onto softball in college and work leagues. I was an average player. I could catch a ball thrown to me and punch one to the opposite field for a single. That, in these leagues, was enough to label me competent.

In all my years of playing ball from Pee Wee League on up, I had only one true regret. I had never hit a home run. Never. Not in Little League, not in Babe Ruth ball. Not in high school or in American Legion contests. I never even slugged one over a fence in a Saturday afternoon pickup game with kids three years younger.

So while other guys from our church were, no doubt, contemplating the friendships they would forge and the lessons to be learned during study and prayer time, I spent the week leading up to the retreat debating whether an out-of-shape, slowed-down forty-one-year-old dreamer still had a few good swings left in him. In the end, I decided to play anyway.

But somewhere along the line, through the years, I lost my glove and never bothered to replace it. On the day of the game, then, I was immediately at a disadvantage. I was a left-hander in need of a glove, which is akin to being a Christian in a synagogue trying to track down a New Testament. I was amazed when Chris, a new acquaintance, produced a small lefty mitt that belonged to his son. Even though this was to be a friendly game, I proceeded to warn my teammates that it had been decades since I had played seriously, that I was slow and required a fairly immobile defensive position

In all my years of playing ball from Pee Wee League on up, I had only one true regret. I had never hit a home run.

if I were to stay this side of a heart attack. I also thought about looking into the possibility of a designated runner for my times at bat but figured that request might place premature strain on my newfound friendships.

We ended up playing three games. The guys were gracious. They put me at catcher and later at first base, the two positions requiring the mobility of a lawn jockey. I surprised everyone with my potent bat. While many were swinging for the fences and flying out deep to the warning track, I was content to punch my patented singles through the hole between first and second into right field. As the day wound on I found myself batting around .700, a good average even in slow-pitch. My joints were aching, and I knew my long-neglected body would present me with an unpayable bill come morning. Still, I was having the time of my life!

As dinnertime was nearing, I approached the batter's box for what I knew would be my last time that day and, who knows, maybe after this we'd call it a career. I took a couple half cuts awaiting the pitch and noticed the outfield defense playing me unusually shallow. One player looked more like the second baseman's shadow than a right fielder. Somebody had been studying my technique. Somebody was challenging me.

As the ball, in its tedious underhanded arc, left the pitcher's hand, I instinctively shifted my feet and changed my stance. I now placed every one of my 280 pounds on my right foot, leaned back, and swung, shattering time and space with the force of my blow.

The eight-millimeter camera in my mind recorded the rest of the event in slow motion. The right fielder looked up in horror and lost his glasses, turning his back to the plate. His steps were high and plodding. The runner on first took off like a gazelle, rounding second and heading for the promised land.

My legs were buoys. They were goalposts stuck in the mud. My thighs were pistons pumping ten-year-old sludge. I could hardly move, but I knew I must. This was my moment. I was halfway to first when the *Petticoat Junction* theme song augmented my highlight reel. Something about Uncle Joe moving kind of slow...

The center fielder rushed over to play the ball in deep right-center and flung it into the second baseman on one hop. When the dust had settled, I ended up…on first. The runner ahead of me had scored…from first. I was doubled over, my lungs screaming for air. Everyone was laughing, including, eventually, me. We had all just witnessed the first recorded instance of a man stretching an inside-the-park homer into a single. I stood there on the base, realizing the uniqueness of my achievement. It was a golden moment. And more poignant than I knew. As I looked toward second, I realized it would only take three more singles—four at the most—to bring me home.

Later that evening, Dave Owen, a visiting pastor, continued his weekend sessions with some wonderful teaching. In spite of my poor body, which spent the evening dialing 9-1-1, I was really getting into his message and hearing God's Word resonate throughout it.

Then, in the middle of his time of sharing, sitting alone in the back row, a picture flashed full blown into my mind. In the scene I was standing on first base, doubled over. This was a picture from a few hours before—my world-class single. But it was painful to see from a different perspective. The man was laughing, but the body was sagging and sadly neglected. There was a wistful look as he glanced toward second base.

At that moment tears began streaming down my face. And a voice that could be mistaken for none other pierced the hollow of my heart with these words of promise: *I want to give you second base…and I want to give you third base…and I want to give you home.*

There are so many ways you could interpret what I had heard. Yet to me, there was no mistaking the message. When words like this reverberate off your ribs and pierce your heart, there is nowhere to hide. *You have abused your body,* was His dispatch, *and wasted so much time. You have wanted so much less for yourself than I have for you. When you are ready, we will round those bases together. I want to help you hit your home run.* Though not His actual words, these represented the spirit of His message as it settled over my soul. And every syllable was true.

I still don't know why God loves me or why He chases me down to show me His love. I don't understand why He chooses to use a game with a ball and a bat to speak in the metaphor and vernacular I am most at ease with or why He hasn't run out of patience when I choose to work things out my way instead of His. I do know there are still pieces missing or broken that keep this heart from fully realizing the great joy and bounty God has for me. I do know that the lines of communication are always open and believe that they reach both ways.

Retreating from my memories, I am back at the stadium. The game has gone extra innings, which is fine by me. Unlike almost any place else in the world, you can never stay too long at the ballpark. It's my turn to get the next round of soft drinks. I wonder, following this ballpark diet, how my seatmate will survive an eon, let alone an eternity.

"I think…" I tell God. "I think I'm ready to take a look at second base now…if the offer is still good."

He smiles the smile of One whose offers seldom expire. The crowd alerts us to a hard shot off the left-center fence. We turn in time to see the pinch hitter trudging into second with a stand-up double. He is clearly winded and bent over, hands on knees, recovering from an oxygen deficit. He looks up finally and is smiling. He seems to be staring straight at us and I wonder why. I look at my scorecard to see which player he is, but the number on his uniform is obscured. I can't help but think he looks familiar.

Yes, says my Creator as we watch His kid take a cautious lead off second. *Let's try to round those bases together. We can start right away, if you like.*

For the first time, I have a feeling everything is going to work out according to His plan. As I focus my attention on the runner, I realize it will probably take only two more singles—three at the most—to bring him home.

It is God who works in you to will and to act according to his good purpose.
—*Philippians 2:13*

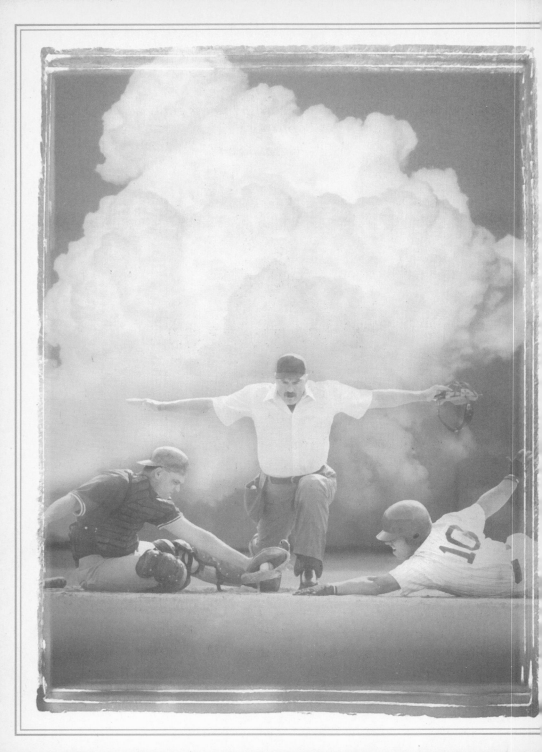

Baseball is like church.
Many attend, but few understand.

—Wes Westrum

Extra Innings

Love Story

The package arrived in a medium-sized brown box, handled by Louie, our UPS driver. I hadn't ordered anything online recently, which prompted my gentle, curious rattling of the contents against the carton's inside walls. Guessing and shaking. Shaking and guessing. When the impromptu test produced no valid data or significant hypothesis, I did what any conscientious man of science would do. I abandoned the experiment and ripped opened the package.

Inside was another container filling most of the first. The tight packing job accounted for the lack of discernible clues. Gift wrapping adorned with logos of thirty Major League Baseball teams enveloped the box in a blatant attempt to curry favor and further the mystery.

It wasn't my birthday or anniversary. In fact, this present arrived outside the jurisdiction of any significant milestone I could think of. I opened it and surveyed its vital organs. Stealth emotion held me hostage for several moments. I set the box down, stood back a respectful distance, and pondered the significance of the contents.

"Wow," I said quietly. It was the only intelligent syllable I could utter.

I paused in nostalgic reflection, then could wait no longer. I was a kid once again and this was Christmas Day. Reaching in with both hands. I was slow—almost reverent—in removing the gift and surveying every surface of its fine brown exterior. I might as well have been handling nitroglycerin for all the care it received.

"Wow," I repeated for effect, "*this* is something."

I grabbed hold of the webbing and slipped the present over my right hand, thick fingers wriggling through leather tunnels they had not entered in years. It was a baseball glove. It was a *broken-in* baseball glove. It was a broken-in baseball glove with a *pocket*. It was a broken-in baseball glove with a pocket, *personally signed* by former major-league catcher Ron Hassey. The significance was not lost on me. Unlike my first glove, this was a mitt you could open and close efficiently with one hand. With a glove like this, a guy had a better than fifty percent chance of catching a ball hit his way. The possibilities were staggering.

I opened and read the note attached: "Just trying to make amends. But no doubt probably fell short again." It was signed, "Love, Dad."

I had recently published "Glove Story" in *The Improbable People Ministries Newsletter*, the free bimonthly mouthpiece our music ministry produces to trumpet our comings and goings. It had been printed with a notice that it was to be part of a book I would be writing for Bethany House Publishers. My father started taking some serious ribbing from my family. Even the local pharmacist, Dan Bertelli, joined in the fun. "Why couldn't you shell out a couple extra bucks for a *real* glove?" had been the general consensus.

And now he had. Thirty-seven years late. But to me, it was right on time.

Pumping the pocket with my fist, I lean into a slight crouch, hands on knees, and wait for a thirty-seven-year-old ball to be hit my way.

I break into a little chatter:

"Hey, batta-batta, batta-batta, suh-WING!"

I look over to the sideline to see if he's come yet. YES—he's just setting up some folding chairs now. Wow, they're *all* here! Dad looks out from under a black and orange hat that has the insignia *SF* sewn on. He waves and I flick my glove in his general direction. Good to see you, Dad.

"Batta-batta, batta-batta. No hit here, batta-batta!"

Sitting next to Dad is Grandpa. Grandpa is taking home movies of the game with which to embarrass us all later. Dad seems to be obliging, making goofy faces and throwing ice cubes at the camera. Why do people degenerate into primates when a lens is pointed in their direction? I must admit, though, I've never seen Dad and Grandpa play like this. My mom is watching too. Must be slow over at the snack bar. She tries to get my attention. Mom, don't *do* this. Don't *embarrass* me. Nobody *else's* mom is waving. I pretend to be immersed in the game.

Pumping the pocket with my fist, I lean into a slight crouch, hands on knees, and wait for a thirty-seven-year-old ball to be hit my way.

Off to the side, just to the left of the chicken-wire backstop, I see God. He seems to be encouraging Hank Waugh, a new kid in the neighborhood. Word is he's a stick. Hank and I might get to be friends. Now God whispers something out to the mound, and our pitcher touches the bill of his cap as if to say thanks. As usual, God seems to be rooting for both teams.

Without word or warning, a high fly ball is heading my way. NASA has it on their radar. The baseball is in orbit around the edge of the sun and I'm having a hard time locating it. *This time it's going to be different,* I think. *This time, I've got my Ron Hassey personally autographed broken-in glove with an actual pocket, and this time I'm gonna catch it.* Even though I'm circling the landing site like a music-box ballerina, I feel pretty good about my chances because I have the newest glove of any guy on the field.

As the ball is descending to the ground, my heart is descending to my stomach. I can see it now. I can *see* it!

"I got it," I shout, as if anyone in his right mind wants a piece of this moonshot. Still, this is what I've been trained to yell. "I got it!"

This time it's going to be different, I think. *This time, I've got my Ron Hassey personally auto- graphed broken-in glove with an actual pocket, and this time I'm gonna catch it.*

The ball hits the center of my glove and bounces away in a high, slow motion arc. Wait a minute! This is *not* how this game is supposed to end. I'm supposed to catch the ball with my dad's new glove and he's going to buy me a Suicide after. That's *it*, I determine. I have dropped my last fly ball.

In mental replays from three cam- era angles the ball hits my mitt and bounds from the springboard of my glove high into the summer sky like an Olympian bounding off the high dive. Wait a minute—of course— that's it! With newfound resolve I fling my body parallel to the ground—my best Roofball dive—and stretch out my gloved hand. The elusive fly ball—the one I've been chasing all my life—is almost within my grasp. *Please, God. Please. Let me catch this one.* The ball hits my pocket and sticks like there's tar in the webbing. Instinctively, I pull the glove into my body to protect the fragile bounty.

I'm laying there and I'm dazed. People are running out on the field to see if I'm all right. And to see if I have the ball. "Nice catch, O'Connor," Hank Waugh shouts as he heads back to the bench from second, after his lunar-orbiting out. "Why don't you come over to my house tomorrow? I've got a new game we could try out."

I start to answer him, but I'm surrounded by those I love. Dad is there shaking hands with the other fathers. Ten games into the season and no one can believe the Raineers have just won their first game. My Grandpa is getting everything on film but manages to give my dad a bear hug while he's shooting. Mom is out there too, making sure I'm not hurt—or worse, dirty.

God is still over by the backstop. He's consoling the Mountaineers and leading them in a 2-4-6-8 cheer for us. I guess I'm a hero. Or at least a reasonable facsimile.

Better get used to it, Michael, God whispers into my heart. *You and I have a lot of years ahead together. And I have only good things in store.*

With those words He is gone from sight, but I'm pretty sure I'll be hearing Him again. Dad comes over and sticks out his hand. "Nice catch, son. I guess I owe you that soda," he says in a mock-grudging tone. "Meet me over at the snack bar in five minutes and I'll pay up."

"OK, Dad," I promise. "I'll be there."

"Say," hollers Dad as he heads over to our Rambler station wagon parked on the street, "looks like that new glove I bought you worked out fine."

"Sure did, Dad," I yell back. But he's already gone.

I'm walking over to the snack bar to collect my reward, and I'm flipping the ball into my new personally signed Ron Hassey broken-in baseball glove with a pocket. But something doesn't feel right. I look down to discover that, in fact, I'm not wearing my personally signed Ron Hassey broken-in glove with a pocket on my right hand at all. I'm wearing—and I can't believe I'm saying this—The Pancake.

I'm staring at my mitt like it came from outer space. There's a permanent oil stain in the middle where a pocket should be and string marks grooved around the edges of both sides. The corners of my mouth bend slowly toward my ears. I can't believe what has happened. I just caught the monster fly ball of a lifetime…and I did it with the flattest glove in creation. My glove. *My* glove.

But why today? How come I had to embarrass myself a million other times before this particular ball found my glove? Check the box score—you won't find it in the agate type. Look in the sporting goods store—you can't buy it with a wad of Ben Franklins.

What was the difference between this and every other botched attempt I ever made at greatness? Turns out it wasn't the glove after all. Imagine that. In the end it was faith, hope, and, most of all, love that brought out the best in me. These are the intangibles you won't find documented in the morning paper. These are the eternal gifts that carried this day.

I get up slowly from my crouch and see the letter in my hand. The correspondence from my dad asking, in his awkward way, forgiveness for a less than perfect judgment a lifetime ago. Fresh drops of my perspiration punctuate the trademark printing I would know anywhere. I reach to wipe the sweat away, but my forehead is bone dry.

It's the only part of my face that is.

You see, Mr. Hanks, no matter how loudly you protest, there is—there *is* crying in baseball.

And God is deeply invested in the game as well. If I didn't know this before, I sure know it now. I believe God loves our national pastime and that He uses it for His own good and holy purposes. I'm living proof.

The funny thing about the two, despite the fact that they are so very different and each is utterly unique, when God decides to use baseball to further His kingdom, reaching out to a heart in desperate need of filling…well…

Youneverknow.

And now these three remain:
faith, hope and love.
But the greatest of these is love.
—*1 Corinthians 13:13*

A Note from the Author

Thank you, friends, for stopping by and leafing through this scrapbook with me. Some of the pictures are worn and faded. Others are as crisp and sharp as the day they were taken. All were preserved with love, and I hope you enjoyed these memories as much as I cherish the opportunity to share them.

When God comes to meet us right where we live, it is an amazing and humbling experience. Just when you get comfortable with the notion that He is constrained by the walls of our congregational buildings, He spills unexpectedly into the labyrinth of streets and highways surrounding our communities.

God knocks on the door of our homes in any number of creative and interesting ways. Then He waits. Even though there hasn't been a church built that can hold Him, neither has there been a front door He's chosen to kick in.

In my case God used baseball as an icebreaker. There was a time I thought mine was the strangest testimony in the world. Then I spoke with a man named Tom who told me the story of how God used the Atlanta Braves to teach him a critical lesson of obedience. I realized in that moment that I was neither strange nor alone.

So I'm wondering if you might have a story to tell of how God has used baseball—or any sport, for that matter—in your life either as a teaching tool or a means to salvation. Would you drop me a line and share your experience with me? I'd love to hear it. Perhaps God has touched you in some special way during our time together. I'd love to hear from you too.

Finally, if you enjoy good Christian music with words that will challenge and sometimes amuse, my wife, Sally, and I would like to invite you to visit our Web site, where you can listen to entire songs, read lyrics and articles we have written, and learn more about the music ministry God has entrusted us with.

I look forward to hearing from you.

Michael O'Connor
Improbable People Ministries
5706 Costello Ave.
Valley Glen, CA 91401
http://www.improbablepeople.org
email: *sermon@improbablepeople.org*

Michael O'Connor

was eight years old when he attended his first Major League baseball game, but he had already developed a respect for the sport that bordered on the sacred. He and his wife now head a national touring music ministry called Improbable People. They live in Southern California with their three children.

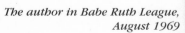

*The author in Babe Ruth League,
August 1969*